1994 North American Fishing Club

Members' Cookbook

Edited by
Ron Larsen
Colleen Ferguson

Design and Typesetting by
Kenneth Kaiser

Published by the North American Fishing Club
Minnetonka, Minnesota 55343

We would like to thank the following for their help:

NAFC Members who contributed their own delicious recipes for this year's Members' Cookbook, and the Hubert Companies of Harrison, Ohio, for contributing some of their excellent fish recipes for use in this year's cookbook which is dedicated to America's magnificent diversity.

NAFC Staff Members including Publisher Mark LaBarbera; *North American Fisherman* Editor Steve Pennaz; Managing Editor, Books Ron Larsen; Associate Editor, Books Colleen Ferguson; Editorial Assistant Victoria Brouillette; Vice President of Product Marketing Mike Vail; Asst. Vice President/Marketing Manager, Books Cal Franklin, and Project Coordinator, Books Jay McNaughton.

Cover illustration contributed by Ken Kaiser; text chapters and regional meals authored by Louis Bignami. Inside photos provided by the author.

Address reprint requests and
orders for additional books to:
NAFC Cookbook Editor
P.O. Box 3403
Minnetonka, MN 55343

The North American Fishing Club offers a line of
fraternal products for members. For information, write:
NAFC, P.O. Box 3408, Minnetonka, MN 55343.

Contents

All The Best Eating, East To West.............................5
by Steve Pennaz, Executive Director

Measures...8

Recipes (Bass-Cod)..9

    Bass 10

    Bluefish...18

    Bonito 19

    Burbot..21

    Butterfish 22

    Carp 24

    Catfish 28

    Chub..32

    Cod..34

The Effette, And Other Easts 37

Meals Of The East...47

Recipes (Crappie-Haddock) 63

    Crappie 64

    Croaker 66

    Crustaceans...68

    Flounder...79

    Froglegs 82

    Grouper..84

    Grunion 86

    Haddock...87

Southern Comforts...89

Meals of the South 99

Recipes (Halibut-Mahi Mahi)............................115

    Halibut...116

    Jack...120

    Lingcod..122

    Mackerel...125

CONTENTS

Mahi Mahi 127
Flat Fishing in the Midwest 129
Meals of the Midwest 139
Recipes (Mollusks-Sole) 153
   Mollusks 154
   Mullet 166
   Perch 168
   Pike 170
   Pollock 171
   Pompano 173
   Rockfish 175
   Roughy, Orange 177
   Salmon 180
   Shark 188
   Smelt 189
   Snapper 192
   Sole 193
Rocky Mountain Highs 195
Meals of the Mountains 203
Recipes (Sturgeon-Walleye) 217
   Sturgeon 218
   Swordfish 220
   Tilapia 223
   Tilefish 225
   Trout 227
   Tuna 235
   Turbot 237
   Walleye 238
Best in the West 243
Meals of the West 251
Recipes (Whitefish-Your Choice) 265
   Whitefish 266
   Whiting 269
   Your Choice 272
Index of Delicious Recipes 281
Contributing Members 288

All The Best Eating, East To West

In the past few years, I have been fortunate enough to fish many locations across North America. The fishing wasn't always great, but the people I met, the sights seen and the lessons learned made every trip a pleasure. The unique qualities that I have found during these trips are the inspiration for the theme of the 1994 NAFC Members' Cookbook that you now hold in your hands.

I fondly recall a fishing trip into Canada that brought this point vividly home to me. We were out on the South Knife River, 100 or so miles west of Churchill, Manitoba, and had been really hitting the pike most of the morning.

Mike Boll and Stuart Webber of Dymond Lake Outfitters were our guides. It was late morning and our stomachs were letting us know it was time to pull into shore for some food.

Mike saved a good-sized pike for our lunch, and started clean-ing and preparing it for cooking while the rest of us attended to other duties. I fully expected him to produce the standard, but delicious, shore lunch of pike, potatoes and beans. Then, he reached into his sack and pulled out green peppers and a rather wide assortment of vegetables. He quickly and efficiently turned all this into a magnificent stir-fry pike meal that was out of this world!

That meal on the bank of the South Knife makes the memory of that fishing trip stand out in my mind—of course, the excellent pike fishing we encountered doesn't hurt, either.

Eating's Next To Fishing
Ask any angler who has traveled to other parts of North America in search of fish, and probably the most frequent answer would be that a major part of the enjoyment comes from discovering the delicious diversity of that area. I don't know many anglers who don't like to eat almost as much as they like to fish.

That's why we asked author Louis Bignami to capture this diver-sity in text, as well as in mouthwatering meals representative of each region. I feel you will agree that he did an exceptionally good job. His coverage of each region reveals a wide selection of complete dinners—from appetizer to dessert—that make each region not only special but unique, as well.

Take some time to read about each and every region—starting with your own—and then check out the meals we've assembled from that region. I'm willing to bet that you can't get through one region without heading for the kitchen and thawing the fillets!

'Firsts' For This Edition
There are several "firsts" associated with this edition. It is the largest NAFC Members' Cookbook to date, both in terms of number of pages (288) and in total number of recipes (over 330). Also, it is the first NAFC cookbook to carry entire meals. Now you can use the cookbook for your entire meal planning, and get better acquainted with the tastes of other regions. I'd call that a real lunker of a cookbook; wouldn't you?

Lou's stories about the five regions—East, South, Midwest,

Mountains and West—are a major bonus. His description of how anglers used to get to their fishing destinations—by railroad—was especially interesting to me. It's hard to imagine today, but in those days the train was the usual way of getting about—for fishermen and everyone else. And then there is the description of the "boat trains" that allowed anglers in rowboats to gain greater lake coverage before the development of the gas-powered motorboat.

Tempting The Tastebuds

Then he leads off the meals with a dinner built around grilled sea bass! That's why I know you won't be able to read through a region without heading for the kitchen.

You will have the same problem getting through the rest of the regions. Just wait until you savor the fish and shrimp crepes that form the heart of a southern meal called "Creole Confections." And it's topped off with Apple Normandy for dessert. The Midwest may have a "meat and potatoes" image, but the broiled walleye with mustard sauce dinner will change that.

Now, on to the mountains. Just wait until you've tried "Nutty-Fried Trout," the "Enchilada Pesca" or the "Cornish Fish Pasties." Then it's on into the West with its "Lingcod Nicoise" with a "Coffee Nut Tortoni" for dessert, or the Dressed Dungeness Crab or the ... Well, I think you get the idea. This cookbook will be fun, filling and satisfying. I guarantee it!

Steve

Steve Pennaz
Executive Director
North American Fishing Club

Cookbook Abbreviations

tsp.	=	teaspoon
T.	=	tablespoon
pt.	=	pint
oz.	=	ounce
lb.	=	pound
pkg.	=	package

Measurement Conversions

1 pinch	=	less than 1/8 tsp.
1 T.	=	3 tsp.
2 T.	=	1 oz.
4 T.	=	$1/4$ cup
5 T. + 1 tsp.	=	$1/3$ cup
8 T.	=	$1/2$ cup
10 T. + 2 tsp.	=	$2/3$ cup
12 T.	=	$3/4$ cup
16 T.	=	1 cup

1 cup	=	8 oz.
1 pint	=	16 oz.
1 quart	=	32 oz.
1 gallon	=	128 oz.

1 cup	=	$1/2$ pint
2 cups	=	1 pint
4 cups	=	1 quart
2 pints	=	1 quart
4 pints	=	$1/2$ gallon
8 pints	=	1 gallon
4 quarts	=	1 gallon
8 gallons	=	1 bushel

Recipes For:

Bass

Bluefish

Bonito

Burbot

Butterfish

Carp

Catfish

Chub

Cod

Deep-Fried Fish

Serves: several
Prep Time: 45 minutes

>   **bass fillets**
> **1**   **cup dry onion-ring mix**
> **³/₄** **cup water**
>   **cooking oil**

Combine onion-ring mix and water to form batter. Dip fillets in batter to coat. Drop fillets into deep-fat fryer heated to 375 degrees. Fry for 2¹/₂-5 minutes, depending upon thickness of fillet. When fish rises to surface of fat, remove fillet with slotted spoon. Drain on paper towels. Serve hot.

Thomas Schaad
Leawood, Kansas

Grilled Or Baked Largemouth Bass

Serves: several
Prep Time: 20-30 minutes

>   **largemouth bass fillets**
> **1-2** **lemons (juice)**
>   **ice cubes**
>   **margarine**

Fillet fish, slicing close to the bone. Turn fillets, flesh-side up, and place in pan. Cover fillets with ice cubes and squeeze juice from fresh lemons over iced fillets. Dot fish with margarine. Grill over hot coals or bake in moderate oven. Serve with melted butter, lemon wedges and white wine.

Tender Baked Bass

Serves: 4
Prep Time: 20-25 minutes

- **4 bass fillets**
- **¹/₂ tsp. salt**
- **¹/₂ cup milk**
- **¹/₂ cup dry bread crumbs**
- **3 T. butter, melted**
- **1 lemon, quartered**

Combine salt and milk in shallow dish. Dip bass into milk mixture and coat with bread crumbs. Place fillets on well-greased baking sheet and pour butter over them. Bake at 350 degrees for 10-12 minutes or until fish is flaky and tender. Garnish with fresh lemon quarters.

The Best Stuffed Bass

Serves: 6
Prep Time: 1 hour

- **1 3-lb. bass, dressed**
- **1¹/₂ cups soft bread crumbs or**
- **1¹/₂ cups rice, cooked**
- **¹/₂ cup onion, chopped**
- **¹/₂ cup celery, chopped**
- **2 T. fresh parsley, minced**
- **1 egg, beaten**
- **1 T. sage, minced**
- **¹/₂ tsp. salt**
- **¹/₈ tsp. paprika**
- **¹/₂ tsp. dried dill**
- **2 T. capers, drained**
- **3 T. butter, melted**

Combine all ingredients, except fish, and mix thoroughly. Place stuffing in cavity of fish and put fish in lightly oiled baking dish. Bake at 325 degrees for 40 minutes or until fish is flaky and tender when tested with fork.

Micro-Easy Bianco Bass

Serves: 6
Prep Time: 30-40 minutes

1	**3-lb. bass (whole), cleaned**
1/2	**tsp. salt**
1/4	**tsp. pepper, freshly ground**
2	**garlic cloves, crushed**
2	**fresh parsley sprigs, chopped**
5	**fresh mint sprigs, chopped**
2	**fresh oregano sprigs, chopped**
1	**cup white or semi-sweet wine**
1/4	**cup water**
	grapes (optional)

Rub inside of fish with salt and pepper. Stuff with garlic, parsley, mint and oregano. Tie fish closed with string to retain its shape. Place fish in deep, 4-qt. microwave-safe casserole. Pour wine and water over fish. Cover tightly. Microwave on high for 10-12 minutes or until center of fish begins to flake when tested with fork. Turn fish once during cooking time. Let stand (covered) for 5 minutes. Remove fish to serving platter and garnish with additional mint sprigs or grapes. Reserved cooking liquid may be spooned over fish, if desired.

Micro-Easy Orange Butter Sea Bass

Serves: 4
Prep Time: 20 minutes

1 1/2-2 lbs. sea bass, fillets
      salt and pepper to taste
  2 T. grated orange zest
  2 tsp. grated lemon zest
  2 T. scallions (white part only), minced
1 1/2 T. fresh parsley, chopped
  6 T. unsalted butter
 1/2 cup orange juice
      parsley sprigs and orange slices

Butter shallow baking dish large enough to hold fish in single layer. Season fish on both sides with salt and pepper; arrange in baking dish. Combine orange and lemon zest, scallions and parsley; sprinkle evenly over fish. Dot with butter and pour orange juice alongside fish. Cover tightly with plastic wrap and microwave on high for 5-8 minutes or until center of fish flakes easily when tested with fork. Baste fish twice during cooking time with orange juice. Let stand (covered) for 5 minutes. Remove fish to serving platter and garnish with parsley and orange slices. Serve with pan juices, if desired.

Broiled Sea Bass With Rarebit Sauce

Serves: 4
Prep Time: 30-40 minutes

2	lbs. sea bass, cut into steaks
	oil
3	T. margarine
1	T. flour
1/2	cup milk
1/2	cup half-and-half
1	T. white wine
1	T. Worcestershire sauce
1/2	tsp. dry mustard
1/4	tsp. paprika
1/4	tsp. cayenne pepper
1 1/2	cups sharp Cheddar cheese, shredded
	carrots curls (optional)
	parsley sprigs (optional)

Preheat broiler. Arrange bass steaks on lightly oiled broiler pan.
Dot with 2 T. margarine. Broil 6 inches from heat for 5 minutes on
one side. Turn and broil for 5 minutes longer on other side or
until fish is tender and flakes easily when tested with fork. Cut
each steak in half and transfer to platter; keep warm. To make
sauce, melt 1 T. butter in medium saucepan. Add flour and cook,
stirring often over moderate heat for 1 minute. Whisk in milk and
half-and-half. Bring to a boil; reduce heat to low and simmer for
5-10 minutes, whisking occasionally, until sauce is thickened and
smooth. Season with Worcestershire sauce, mustard, paprika
and cayenne pepper. Add cheese and stir until smooth. Spoon
sauce over fish and garnish with carrot curls and fresh parsley
sprigs.

Cranberry-Stuffed Bass

Serves: 4-6
Prep Time: 1 hour

2-3	**white large bass**
	salt to taste
	paprika to taste
1	**apple, peeled, cored and chopped**
1	**lemon (juice) and rind, grated**
1	**cup rice (cooked)**
1/2	**cup whole-berry cranberry sauce**
1/4	**tsp. celery salt**
1/4	**tsp. onion powder**
2	**T. parsley, chopped**
1	**egg, well-beaten**
1/4	**cup butter, melted**

Scale and clean bass thoroughly and slit belly. Season fish, inside and outside, with salt and paprika. Combine apple, lemon rind, rice, cranberry sauce, celery salt, onion powder, parsley and egg to make stuffing. Stuff fish cavity with this mixture. Sew or skewer close the opening. Place fish in greased baking pan lined with aluminum foil. Combine lemon juice and butter; brush over fish. Bake fish at 350 degrees for 40 minutes or until golden brown and fish flakes easily. Carefully place fish on warmed serving platter and remove skewers. Garnish with parsley and thin lemon slices. Small glazed carrots and whipped potatoes make excellent side dishes.

Leo Seffelaar
Tantallon, Saskatchewan

Garlic Broiled Bass

Serves: 3-4
Prep Time: 20-25 minutes

4-5 **small bass**
3 **fresh garlic cloves, minced**
2/3 **cup olive oil**
2 **tsp. salt**
1/2 **cup fresh parsley**
fresh lemon juice

Arrange bass in shallow baking pan. Sprinkle with garlic, olive oil, salt and half of parsley. Broil 4 inches from heat source for 5-7 minutes on each side. Sprinkle remaining parsley and lemon juice over fish. Serve.

David Glossenger
Honesdale, Pennsylvania

Micro-Easy Bay Blue Chowder

Serves: 4
Prep Time: 45 minutes

2	lbs. bluefish, cut into bite-sized chunks	1/4	cup flour
8	bacon slices	1	tsp. dried parsley flakes
1/2	cup onion, chopped	4	cups half-and-half
1/2	cup celery, chopped		salt and pepper
1	tsp. dried seafood seasoning		dash paprika
2	cups frozen hash-brown potatoes		

Place bacon in deep, 3-qt. casserole and cover with paper towels. Microwave on high for 6-8 minutes or until bacon is crisp. Remove, reserving 1/4 cup drippings in casserole. Add onion, celery, seasoning and potatoes to casserole. Cover and microwave on high for 4-5 minutes or until tender. Stir in flour and parsley, blending well. Add half-and-half, salt and pepper and fish. Microwave on high for 12-14 minutes, stirring frequently. (Do not boil.) Garnish with crumbled bacon and paprika before serving.

Fried Bluefish Fillets

Serves: 2
Prep Time: 30 minutes

2	bluefish fillets	butter
1	egg	lemon wedges or tartar sauce
	bread crumbs	

In bowl, beat egg. Dip fillets in egg to coat both sides then roll in bread crumbs. Melt butter in frying pan and add fish. Cook on low heat for about 5 minutes on each side until coating is brown. Serve with lemon wedges or tartar sauce.

Andrew Banchanski
Edison, New Jersey

Grilled Bluefish With Vegetable Vinaigrette

Serves: 4-8
Prep Time: 1 hour, 30 minutes

1   4-8 lb. whole bluefish, dressed
1/3 cup bottled Italian dressing
      fresh ground black pepper
2   lemons, thinly sliced
      oil

Brush fish with salad dressing and pepper; arrange lemon slices in fish cavity. Prepare grill, making sure fire is hot and briquets banked. Brush oil over exterior of fish and place fish in fish basket. Place basket 4-6 inches from heat over banked coals. Cover and cook for 10-12 minutes per inch of thickness. Turn fish once and reapply oil. Cook unitl fish flakes easily when tested with fork. Arrange on serving platter and garnish with marinated and drained vegetables and parsley sprigs.

Oriental Bonito Stir-Fry

Serves: 4
Prep Time: 30-45 minutes

1	lb. bonito chunks	2	cups mushrooms, sliced
1/2	cup wine		
1	tsp. ginger	1/2	cup celery, sliced
2	cloves garlic, minced	1/2	cup green onion, chopped
1/2	tsp. onion powder		
1/2	tsp. pepper	1	cup broccoli, sliced
2	tsp. sugar	1	cup snow peas
1	T. soy sauce		toasted sesame seeds (optional)
1	T. oil		

Combine wine, ginger, garlic, onion powder, pepper, sugar and soy sauce to form marinade. Add bonito and marinate for 15 minutes. Heat oil in wok or large skillet. Add mushrooms, celery, onion, broccoli and snow peas and stir-fry until tender. Add fish and marinade; cook until fish is tender and flaky. Sprinkle toasted sesame seeds over top and serve.

Quick Oven-Poached Bonito

Serves: 4
Prep Time: 30-45 minutes

1	lb. bonito steaks or fillets	1	onion, sliced
4	cups water	2	carrots, sliced
1/2	cup tarragon vinegar	1/2	celery stalk, sliced
2	bay leaves	1/2	tsp. salt
6	peppercorns		

In saucepan, combine water, vinegar, bay leaves, peppercorns, onion, carrots, celery and salt; simmer. Arrange fish in 9x13-inch baking pan at least 2 inches deep. Pour liquid over fish and cover pan tightly with aluminum foil. Bake at 400 degrees for 20 minutes or until fish is tender and flaky. Carefully remove bonito from liquid and serve hot or cold.

Bayland Brochettes

Serves: 4
Prep Time: 1 hour

1	lb. bonito, cut into 2-inch chunks
1/4	cup fresh lemon juice
	bay leaves
8	peppercorns
1/2	tsp. salt
2	medium red onions, quartered
	cherry tomatoes
2	lemons, quartered

In medium bowl, combine fish, lemon juice, bay leaves, pepper-corns and salt. Cover and refrigerate for 30 minutes, turning frequently. Thread 4 skewers alternately with fish, onion, tomatoes, lemon wedges and bay leaves to make brochettes. Preheat oven and place brochettes on rack in pan 4 inches from heat. Broil for 8-10 minutes. Brush with marinade every 3 minutes. Remove and serve with hot rice.

Burbot Fish

Serves: 4
Prep Time: 30-45 minutes

- **2 cups uncooked burbot, cut into chunks**
- **4 T. butter**
- **1/4 cup dry sherry**
- **1/4 teaspoon salt**
- **2 eggs, beaten**
- **1 cup cream**
- **dash cayenne pepper**

Melt butter in top of double boiler. Add sherry and fish chunks. Heat slowly for about 5-10 minutes until wine evaporates. Add salt and leave over hot water. Blend beaten eggs into cream and stir into fish mixture. Add cayenne pepper. Cook and stir over moderate heat until sauce thickens. (Do not boil.)

Leo Seffelaar
Tantallon, Saskatchewan

Quick Broiled Butterfish With Lemon Glaze

Serves: 4-6
Prep Time: 1 hour, 30-45 minutes

2 lbs. butterfish fillets
1 medium lemon, grated and juiced
1/4 cup brown sugar
1/4 tsp. ground nutmeg
3 T. oil

Glaze:
3 T. frozen lemonade concentrate
3 T. water
2 T. cornstarch
fresh mint sprigs

In shallow dish, combine lemon, brown sugar, nutmeg and oil to form marinade. Marinate fillets in refrigerator for 1 hour, turning once. Remove fish, strain and reserve marinade. Place fish on lightly oiled broiler pan and broil 6 inches from heat for 5-7 minutes or until fish flakes when tested with fork. To make glaze, add lemonade concentrate, water and cornstarch to reserved marinade in small saucepan. Blend well, dissolving all lumps. Bring mixture to a boil for 2 minutes or until mixture thickens. Spoon hot glaze over fillets and garnish with fresh mint sprigs.

Burgundy Baked Butterfish

Serves: 2-4
Prep Time: 1 hour

2^1/$_2$	**lbs. butterfish**
1	**large onion, sliced**
	butter or oil
1	**small zucchini, sliced**
	salt and pepper to taste
^{3}/$_4$	**cup bread crumbs**
3	**T. butter**

Marinade:

^{1}/$_2$	**tsp. salt**
1	**bay leaf, whole**
^{1}/$_2$	**tsp. dried thyme**
2	**T. fresh lemon juice**
1^1/$_2$	**cup red burgundy wine**

Rinse whole butterfish and cut crosswise into 4-5 pieces; place in bowl. Combine all marinade ingredients and marinate fish for 3-4 hours. In small pan, saute onion in butter or oil. In baking dish large enough to hold fish, arrange onion and sliced zucchini. Season with salt and pepper. Remove fish from marinade and place on top of vegetable mixture. Remove bay leaf and pour marinade over fish. Sprinkle bread crumbs over top and bake at 425 degrees for 10 minutes. Melt 3 T. butter and brush lightly over fish. Bake for 10 more minutes. Brush fish again with remaining butter and bake for 20 minutes or until fish flakes when tested with fork.

Gefilte Fish

Serves: 10
Prep Time: 3 hours

1	lb. carp
1	lb. whitefish
1	lb. pike
1	onion
1	celery stalk
1/4	cup fresh parsley, chopped
2	eggs, beaten
1/4	cup matzo meal or crushed crackers
1/2	tsp. salt
1/4	tsp. pepper
1	cup water, chilled
	boiling water

Remove skin and bones from fish and blend in food processor along with onion, celery and parsley. Stir in eggs, matzo meal or crackers, salt and pepper. Cover and chill for at least 30 minutes. Dip hands in chilled water and form fish mixture into 1-inch balls. Gently drop balls into large saucepan of boiling water and simmer (uncovered) for 30 more minutes. Remove balls with slotted spoon and chill.

Carp Swimming In Sweet And Sour Sauce

Serves: 4
Prep Time: 30-40 minutes

3	lbs. carp, cleaned and cubed
1/3	cup brown sugar
6-7	T. cornstarch
1/3	cup white wine vinegar
3/4	cup chicken bouillon
3	tsp. soy sauce
5	T. sherry
1 1/2	tsp. fresh ginger, minced
1	garlic clove, minced
1/2	cup bamboo shoots, thinly sliced
	oil
1	green pepper, julienned
3	green onions, cut into 2-inch-long pieces

To make sweet and sour sauce, combine sugar, 1 1/2 T. corn-starch, vinegar, bouillon, 2 tsp. soy sauce, 2 T. sherry, ginger, garlic and bamboo shoots in small saucepan. Bring to a boil, stirring constantly. Reduce heat, cover and keep warm over low heat. Combine 3 T. sherry and 1 tsp. soy sauce and brush over fish. Lightly coat fish with cornstarch. In large frying pan, heat 1/2 inch oil to 360 degrees. Cook fish for about 2-3 minutes on each side or until skin is crusty and fish flakes easily. Add green pepper and onions to sweet and sour sauce and pour over fish.

Bohemian Gypsy Carp

Serves: 4-6
Prep Time: 1 hour, 20 minutes

2	lbs. carp fillets, skinned
	salt to taste
2	bacon strips, diced
2-3	onions, minced
1/4	tsp. dill seed
1/2	tsp. paprika
	butter
3	T. cooking sherry
1	cup sour cream
	fresh parsley

Cut carp into serving-sized pieces. Sprinkle salt on all sides of fish and let stand for 30 minutes. Meanwhile, fry bacon and dice. Add onions, dill seed and paprika. Brown carp pieces, stirring occasionally. Butter loaf pan lavishly and spread one layer of fish in bottom after shaking salt from each piece. Add layer of onion-bacon mixture, another layer of carp and top with remaining onion-bacon mixture. Mix sherry into sour cream. Pour sherry-cream mixture over top of fish and return to oven for 5 minutes. Garnish with fresh parsley. Serve with baked potatoes.

Leo Seffelaar
Tantallon, Saskatchewan

Carp Patties

Serves: 4
Prep Time: 20 minutes

> **2 cups carp, cooked and flaked**
> **1 cup cracker crumbs**
> **1/4 onion, chopped**
> **2 eggs**
> **salt and pepper to taste**
> **cooking oil**
> **lemon juice or tartar sauce**

In medium mixing bowl, combine carp, cracker crumbs, onion, eggs and salt and pepper. Fry in hot oil until golden brown. Serve with lemon juice or tartar sauce.

Sarah King
Wagoner, Oklahoma

Catfish With Creole Sauce

Serves: 4-6
Prep Time: 1 hour

- **6**   **catfish fillets**
- **1**   **tsp. garlic, minced**
- **1**   **tsp. paprika**
- **1**   **tsp. dried tarragon, crumbled**

Creole Sauce:
- **2**   **T. margarine**
- **1/2**   **cup onion, chopped**
- **1/2**   **cup green pepper, chopped**
- **1/2**   **cup okra, thinly sliced**
- **1**   **16-oz. can tomatoes (with liquid)**
- **2**   **T. tomato paste**
- **1**   **cup tomato juice**
-   **cayenne pepper to taste**
- **1/2**   **tsp. salt**
- **1¹/2**   **tsp. sugar**

Season catfish with garlic, paprika and tarragon. Place fillets on cookie sheet and cook until fish flakes easily when pierced with fork. To make Creole sauce, melt margarine in heavy saucepan. Add onion, green pepper and okra. Cook, stirring frequently, until onion is tender. Cut up tomatoes and add with liquid. Add remaining ingredients and stir well. Bring sauce to a boil, then simmer for 10 minutes.

Baked Catfish

Serves: 2
Prep Time: 30 minutes

1-2	**lbs. catfish fillets**
	water
	margarine or butter
1/2	**cup dry onion-ring mix or**
1/4	**cup per lbs. of fish**

Moisten fish with water; set aside. Melt butter or margarine in shallow pan. Pour onion ring mix into plastic bag. Put fillets into bag and shake to coat. Arrange coated fish in single layer in pan. Turn immediately to coat both sides of fish with margarine. Bake at 350 degrees for 15-20 minutes.

Thomas Schaad
Leawood, Kansas

Cheesy Catfish, Please!

Serves: 8
Prep Time: 30-40 minutes

2	**lbs. catfish fillets, skinned**
1/4	**cup Parmesan cheese**
1/4	**cup flour**
1/2	**tsp. pepper**
1	**tsp. paprika**
1/4	**cup milk**
2	**T. margarine, melted**
3	**oz. mozzarella, shredded**
3	**oz. cheddar cheese, shredded**

Combine Parmesan cheese, flour, pepper and paprika in bowl. Dip catfish in milk and coat with cheese mixture. Place fish in baking dish and pour margarine over fish. Bake at 400 degrees for 15-20 minutes or until fish is golden and flaky. Mix shredded cheeses together and sprinkle over fish; broil until bubbly.

Micro-Easy Calico Catfish

Serves: 4
Prep Time: 20-30 minutes

1-1¹/₂ lbs. catfish, precooked, poached fillets
      or steaks, cubed
  2   T. butter
  1   medium white potato, pared and cubed
1/4   cup onion, chopped
1¹/₂ cup chicken broth
      (or poaching liquid, strained)
  2   ears corn on the cob, cut into 1-inch pieces
  2   medium tomatoes, peeled and quartered
  1   medium zucchini, cut into 1-inch pieces
1/2   tsp. basil, dried
1/2   tsp. oregano, dried
1/2   tsp. salt

In deep 2-qt. casserole, combine all ingredients except fish. Cover and microwave on high for 10-15 minutes or until vegetables are barely tender, stirring once. Add fish chunks to casserole. Cover and microwave on high for 3-4 minutes or until fish is thoroughly heated.

Catfish Anna

Serves: 3
Prep Time: 40-50 minutes

1-1¹/₂ lbs. catfish fillets
  1 medium onion, thinly sliced
  1 large zucchini, thinly sliced
  1 medium tomato, peeled and thinly sliced
  ¹/₂ tsp. dried oregano
     salt to taste
  ¹/₃ cup white wine or water
  1 cup sour cream
  ²/₃ tsp. mustard
  ¹/₈ tsp. salt
     paprika

Lightly oil 12x8-inch casserole, then alternately line bottom with onion, zucchini and tomatoes slices. Season with oregano and salt (to taste). Place fillets on top of vegetable mixture. Add wine or water. Cover casserole with aluminum foil and bake for 25 minutes or until fish is flaky and tender. Transfer fish to warm oven-proof platter. In small bowl, combine sour cream, mustard and ¹/₈ tsp. salt. Spread sour cream mixture over fish and sprinkle paprika on top. Broil fish for 5 minutes or until topping is brown and bubbly.

Camper's Special

Serves: 4-6
Prep Time: 1 hour, 20-30 minutes

1	lb. smoked chub, skinned, boned and flaked
3-4	red potatoes, sliced
2	T. oil
1	T. fresh basil, finely chopped
1/2	tsp. salt
1/4	tsp. fresh ground pepper
1	small red onion, diced

Boil sliced potatoes (don't peel) for 8-10 minutes or until almost tender in large saucepan of salted water. Drain well. Add remaining ingredients and mix gently. Let stand for 1 hour and serve at room temperature.

Micro-Easy Creamed Chub With Capers

Serves: 4
Prep Time: 15 minutes

1	lb. chub, cooked and flaked	1/4	tsp. paprika
1/4	cup butter or margarine	1	cup milk
1/4	cup flour	1	cup green peas (optional)
1/4	tsp. salt	2	T. capers
1	T. fresh parsley, minced		

Place butter or margarine in glass bowl and cover. Microwave on high for 45 seconds. With whisk, blend flour, salt and paprika. Microwave on high for 30 seconds. Whisk milk into mixture and microwave on high for 3-3$1/2$ minutes (do not boil). Add chub, peas and capers. Heat on high for 1-2 minutes. Sprinkle fresh parsley on top of fish and serve over buttered noodles or toast.

Chubby Checkers

Serves: 4
Prep Time: 45 minutes

2	**cups chub, flaked**
2¹/₂	**cups tomatoes, peeled, seeded and chopped**
1	**green pepper, chopped**
3	**cups soft bread crumbs**
2	**T. butter**
¹/₄	**cup onion, chopped**
¹/₂	**tsp. salt**
1	**tsp. sugar**
¹/₄	**tsp. paprika**
1	**egg, beaten**
1	**tsp. lemon juice**
¹/₄	**cup white wine**
¹/₂	**cup cheddar cheese, grated**

Combine tomatoes, green pepper and 1¹/₂ cups bread crumbs; set aside. In separate bowl, combine fish with remaining ingredients (except cheese). In greased casserole, alternate fish and tomato mixtures into checkerboard pattern. Top with cheese. Bake at 375 degrees for 15 minutes or until golden on top and heated thoroughly.

Easy Portuguese Cod

Serves: 4
Prep Time: 20-30 minutes

4	cod fillets	1	fresh thyme sprig
1/8	tsp. pepper	3	tomatoes, peeled,
1	onion, finely chopped		seeded and chopped
1	garlic clove, minced	1/2	cup white wine
1/4	cup fresh parsley, minced	1/4	tsp. salt

Season cod with pepper and place fish in large skillet. Add remaining ingredients and bring to a boil. Reduce heat and simmer (covered) for 10 minutes. Carefully remove cod and keep warm. Continue to cook tomato mixture for another 5 minutes. Pour mixture over fish and serve immediately.

Bite-Sized Cod Balls

Serves: several (yields 2-3 dozen)
Prep Time: 1 hour

1 1/2	lbs. cod fillets, finely chopped	1/2	tsp. fish seasoning
1/2	cup milk	1	tsp. dried parsley
1/2	cup water		salt and pepper to taste
1/2	butter	1	cup flour
4	eggs		

In medium saucepan, combine milk, water, butter, fish seasoning, parsley and salt and pepper. Heat until almost boiling. Add flour and cook until mixture forms a ball. Remove from heat and allow to cool slightly. Add eggs, one at a time, beating well after each addition. Blend in minced cod. (Pastry batter should be stiff.) Drop by teaspoonfuls onto greased baking sheet. Bake at 450 degrees for 10 minutes; reduce heat to 350 degrees and bake for an additional 10 minutes. Serve hot with tarter sauce.

Codfish Balls

Serves: 4
Prep Time: 30 minutes

1	cup cod, cooked and flaked	1/4	tsp. salt	
1 1/2	cups mashed potatoes	1/8	tsp. pepper	
1	egg, beaten	1/2	tsp. onion juice (optional)	
1	T. butter, melted hot sauce (optional)		cooking oil	

Combine all ingredients (except hot sauce) and blend until smooth and fluffy. Lightly shape mixture into balls or cakes. Fry in deep fat at 375 degrees until brown. Serve with hot sauce.

John Gagliardo
Oxnard, California

Micro-Easy Classic Cod Chowder

Serves: 4-6
Prep Time: 1 hour

1	lb. cod fillets, drained and diced	1/4	cup flour
8	bacon slices, chopped	1/4	tsp. salt
1	cup raw potatoes, peeled and diced	4 1/2	cups light cream or half-and-half
1/2	cup onion, chopped		fresh parsley sprigs

Place bacon in deep, 3-qt. casserole; cover with paper towels. Microwave bacon on high for 6-8 minutes until crisp. Drain bacon, crumble and set aside. Reserve 1/4 cup bacon drippings and add potatoes and onion. Cover and microwave on high for 7-8 minutes or until tender. Stir in flour and salt until well-blended; add cream, mixing well. Add diced cod and microwave on high for 12-14 minutes, stirring frequently, until mixture begins to boil and thicken. (Do not boil.) Reduce heat to medium and cook for 3-4 minutes for additional thickening. Garnish each serving with crumbled bacon and fresh parsley sprigs.

Cathy's Pan-Fried Fish Parmesana

Serves: 4
Prep Time: 25-35 minutes

- **2 lbs. cod**
- **1 T. lemon juice**
- **1 T. Worcestershire sauce**
- **salt and pepper to taste**
- **1/2 cup flour**
- **3 eggs, lightly beaten**
- **1 cup Parmesan cheese, grated**
- **3 T. butter**
- **2 T. canola oil**

Combine lemon juice and Worcestershire sauce; sprinkle mixture over fish pieces. Add salt and pepper to taste. Lightly dredge fish in flour. Dip fish in eggs; then lightly coat with flour. Dip fish in eggs again and coat generously with grated cheese. In heavy skillet, melt butter and oil. Saute fish over medium heat for 3-4 minutes until brown; turn and brown other side. Place skillet in oven for 4-5 minutes to heat thoroughly. Serve immediately.

Steve Schlerf
Hydesville, California

Meals Of The East

The Effette, And Other Easts

Fishing history of the East is really the history of fishing in America. No other area has influenced angling as much as this part of the country. With its early British roots in upper crust field sports, healthy dash of German, French and Scandinavian techniques and unique mix of species, the East once had it all. American fly fishing for brook, brown and other trout started here. Surfcasting, plug fishing for pike and muskies, trolling for bluefish, saltwater fly and light tackle fishing and many other fishing techniques developed in the East.

You can make a good case that saltwater fishing for cod settled New England. Hard-headed English and French natives settled near the superb fishing along the Atlantic Coast. It wasn't long until French boats started fishing Canadian waters—just 12 years after Columbus discovered the Americas! Settlers quickly established supply and fish processing centers in the Gulf of St. Lawrence. Some suggest these fish processing systems with specialized headers, gutters and splitters was the first assembly line in the new world.

By the early 1600s the British had over 25 boats on the Grand and other banks—the productive shallows in the Atlantic where cod school up to spawn so aptly portrayed in Kipling's Captains Courageous and the Spencer Tracy film. John Smith, the beloved of Indian maidens, claimed in his Description Of New England that "you'd have to be a bad fisher not to take two or three hundred cod a day."

Today, you could probably walk across the water on striper or bluefish boats moored to fish in these areas!

Smith also reported catching 62 sturgeon at one time in a net, and other accounts tell us that sturgeon jumped in Boston Harbor well into the 1800s. By about the time of the Revolutionary War, reports of 5,000 shad taken in one seine weren't uncommon. Salmon were so plentiful that farmers that went to rivers to buy shad for feed and fertilizer had to take an equal amount of salmon. Fish were commonly fed to cattle in Provincetown and flounders were used mostly for lobster bait. Lobster were even used for cod bait. Indentured servants, who traded their labor for a period of years for a ticket to the New World, complained bitterly about eating ducks, striped bass, salmon and lobsters instead of "good British beef and mutton."

Saltwater Sports

Sportfishing in saltwater started early. We know George Washington fished off Sandy Hook near Long Island and off the New Hampshire Coast, and fly fishermen got into the act in the 1800s. As they sought sea-run brook trout in the mouths of Long Island streams, striped bass hit their streamers; however, most sportfishermen remained wedded to the freshwater fish. Many found trout on Manhattan or nearby. But even then anglers knew bigger fish finned the St. Lawrence and Maine lakes.

H.W. Herbert, who wrote under the pseudonym Frank Forester, was America's first major outdoor writer. His varied interests lured Americans out of their dependence on European field sports and placed the focus on freshwater fly fishing.

Forester, who popularized fly fishing for trout, bass, shad and even herring, also noted the multiple joys of fishing for bluefish, weakfish, striped bass and more arcane saltwater species like sharks. It's fair to state he popularized recreational, as opposed to sustenance, fishing in the United States.

Before The Civil War

Fishermen found shared interest in specific species. Clubs formed to troll up bluefish in the early 1800s when small cat boats were used. Surf fishing began in the 1840s with fragile piers built out from shore for the gentry who could leave the mundane chores of chumming and gaffing fish to paid assistants. Other clubs employed harpooners to spear porpoises and used specially built sailboats to reach inshore grounds. At this time, fishermen had discovered Maine and its 5- to 10-pound brook trout, the Atlantic salmon waters north of dammed rivers and the joys of St. Lawrence bass. "Cottages" like the monster establishments still looming over the cliffs of Newport, Rhode Island, offered local employment as logging decimated forests.

The Maine Guide boat, perhaps the most effective "people-powered" freshwater fishing craft until the development of West Coast McKenzie River boats, let the gentle folk lounge in the stern while the tough Maine watermen handled details like rowing and shore lunches. Trout still ran in Long Island streams, and a growing network of railroads, plus the Robber Baron's flotilla of private rail cars, let the fishermen of the day escape close to home waters.

Improvements in linen line caused booms in surfcasting with massive Calcutta rods, brass reels sans drags and anti-reverses and huge rigged eels or squids. Even before automobiles, anglers weren't stuck! The Erie Railroad, for example, had listed "several hundred points in New York and Pennsylvania where excellent fishing and hunting may be had."

Small steamers and canal boats increased the angler's mobility in a manner only approached 100 years later when Henry Ford gave anglers private wheels. Nor were costs excessive. Steamer passage from New York City to Albany ran a dollar for adults, and canal boats charged a cent a mile.

Canada beckoned. The British, flushed with cash from their coal mines and the early stages of the Industrial Revolution, crossed the Atlantic and ventured up the St. Lawrence. With fly and spoon they tempted the same Atlantic salmon whose numbers were declining in befouled English waters. The huge brook trout and muskie streams and lakes, coupled with splendid aquatic mobility and a growing network of lodges centered around Quebec, attracted anglers from all over the world. Railroads now offered direct runs to the best waters of New Brunswick and, thanks to a small fleet of 19 knot steamers, Nova Scotia.

The Best

The massive expansion of rail lines and industry in the East after the Civil War changed fishing. More population meant more pressure; much of Maine had been so logged off that timber cutters left to do the same for Michigan and, eventually, the West Coast. Streams dammed to provide power changed from Atlantic salmon haunts to bass waters, and brook trout in the many natural lakes and logging ponds dropped in size. As a result, the action moved down along the coast or upstate into private tracts or even farther north along the St. Lawrence and into Canada.

The technology that won the war for the North improved tackle, too. Reels featured major improvements in bearings, started to multiply and sprouted drags and levelwinds. Lines, which were mostly braided linen, became more uniform and reliable. Hooks, now mass produced, and gut leaders, diamond cut for uniformity, improved results.

Decent bamboo rods which were softer but more forgiving than current graphite material improved fly fishing. Other improvements included aluminum cooking gear, better tents, folding boats and the realization that automobiles could get you there.

Still, modern anglers have little conception of the time it took to maintain gear as late as 1940. Leave a bamboo rod out in the damp and its six sections separated, and reels rusted quickly if they weren't greased. Line was run off reels onto massive wooden dryers where it was rinsed, then dried. Leaders required soaking. Fly lines, like L.L. Bean boots and coated cotton weatherproofing, needed dressing. Guides earned much of their pay from gear maintenance.

As always, most fished near home. Given the lack of transportation, rental boats were standard and inexpensive. In the East, both canoes and guide boats got the ink. Rather battered flat-bottomed, spay-sided skiffs cobbled up with often green timber seemed more common. All shared two things: lusty leaks and a dipper made from an old can.

On large lakes, "boat trains" offered improved range. A small steamer, often a tiny tug once used to move boomed

Nothing compares to preparing fresh fish right where you caught them as this East Coast angler is doing.

logs, would offer power. Lines of boats filled with anglers would string out with those who lusted for nearby water trailing. Off went the train as boats dropped off the trail and headed toward shore to probe waters for bass and trout. It wasn't until 1886 that Daimler built the first gas-powered motorboat in Germany—one horsepower! Ole Evinrude's lusty one-lungers advertised that they "did not require a rudder" and that "the propeller turns freely in either direction to steer the boat." Claims for hard-rubber reels suggested angler gullibility isn't new.

Century's Turn

National outdoor magazines started to become popular. If you couldn't make an Alaskan trip or chase billfish off Australia, you could read the accounts of those who did. In 1880, trout options expanded with the introduction of

There's a certain elegance to the surf fisherman's long rod arching against the weight of the bait as anglers probe near shore for stripers and other battlers.

brown and rainbow trout into New England waters. After World War I, the best fishing in the Northeast had gone with timber and free flowing streams. Access to some of the best waters had become privatized by clubs.

Population and pollution, along with minimal game management, led to a period in the area's history of "licenses, limits and wanderlust."

Fishing and hunting licenses became common. Fishermen had to search farther for action. Some adventurous types even used a World War I seaplane to reach the Bahamas. Early float planes eased into Canadian waters that offered the peak action.

Between The Wars
The 1920s and '30s offered money to fish and leisure to enjoy it; however, not in the same decades. Big game fishing tackle improved radically with new boat designs.

Evinrudes and other motors had covers and mufflers, and fishermen had better agate guides. Spinning reels were invented in Europe; however, the advances of World War II technology eased casting for everyone. As angler numbers increased, nocturnal fishing became more popular in fresh- and saltwater. Specialized saltwater magazines and anglers popularized coastal action.

The Rest
After the world wars, angling in the Northeast was well-known. As New York, Philadelphia, Boston, Pittsburgh and other population centers in the East expanded, fishing declined. More dams, more pollution, more pressure and the other dubious side effects of industrialization and urbanization radically affected riverine species. Atlantic salmon that once ran into Long Island waters lost most of their American habitat. Striper numbers plummeted, hard hit by problems of Hudson River and Chesapeake Bay

water quality and the abject failure of Eastern states to limit the commercial take. Traditional trout streams like the Neversink and Battenkill where American fly fishing was born got hammered.

Conservation And Concern

Fortunately, fishermen started to make their voices heard. Groups like the International Game Fish Association, Trout Unlimited and the Izaak Walton League joined with general conservation groups. License money let fish and game departments hire more professional biologists and, where not distracted by political pressures, improve habitat.

Clean water and clean air standards started to bring things back. Striper numbers increased with stocking, slot limits, habitat improvements and curtailment of commercial action. Catch-and-release trout waters improved chances to catch decent fish at the price of, in some areas, reservations and fees.

Most species now offer superb action. Pike and even muskies wait in ambush under semi-submerged logs. New species, like tiger or amur muskies or the often despised carp, improve options. But the biggest, most important change in the East is attitude. Trapped in urban and suburban settings, today's anglers understand that an 8-inch brown trout caught and released with the right gear can fuel a day, a week or a season's pleasant memories.

Formal Without Fuss
Serves: 4-6

Quenelles, poached fish cakes if you like, exist in French and most European cuisines. This lovely appetizer also can be served as a formal lunch. Add quick-and-easy grilled bass or, if the budget permits, steamed lobster with a butter-tarragon sauce, some wild rice, a few green beans and a classic desert named for one of New York's favorite opera stars and you have a "drop dead" New England meal to impress the most picky in-laws. A fine French white wine or a special California wine like a Kendall-Jackson chardonnay goes along nicely. So does champagne!

Appetizer: Quenelles

1½	lbs. fish fillets
3	egg whites
1½	cups whipping cream
⅛	tsp. salt
¼	tsp. white pepper
¼	tsp. dillweed

Lobster Sauce:

½	cup cooked lobster, diced
2	T. butter
1	green onion, finely chopped
2	T. flour
1½	cups milk
3	T. whipping cream
	salt and pepper
½	tsp. paprika

Beat egg whites lightly with fork until broken. In food processor or blender, grind fish fillets. Add egg whites and blend a few seconds more or until smooth. Slowly pour in cream and mix until texture is like whipped cream. Stir in salt, pepper and dill-weed and mix well. (Note: Salt will stiffen mixture immediately. Also if kitchen is hot, mixture should be placed in chilled bowl which is inserted in larger bowl of ice while mixing.)

In large shallow pan, add water and bring to a boil. Shape 2-3 T.

of fish mixture into ovals similar in shape to mussels or thin clams. Reduce heat and add quenelles; simmer for 10-12 minutes or until firm. Remove quenelles with slotted spoon and drain carefully on paper towels. Arrange on warm serving dish.

To make lobster sauce, melt butter in saucepan over medium heat. Add green onion and saute until soft. Stir in flour; then add milk and bring to a boil. Reduce heat and simmer for 5 minutes or until sauce thickens. Mix in cream and lobster and cook for 2 more minutes. Do not boil. Season with salt and pepper to taste. Serve sauce over quenelles and sprinkle paprika on top. (Variation: Use cooked, peeled shrimp pieces instead of lobster.)

Entree No.1: Grilled Sea Bass

- **1   5-lb. bass fillet**
- **1   stick butter**
- **1/4   cup your favorite fresh herb mixture (ex. tarragon, basil, chives, parsley cilantro), chopped**

Heat broiler and melt butter over medium heat in sauce pan. Add herbs and cook for about 1 minute. Grill fish skin-side up for 10 minutes, basting with butter. Turn fish over and grill for 5 minutes. Baste fish with butter and grill for 5 more minutes.

Entree No.2: Steamed Lobster

- **1   lobster**
- **salt**

Dump live or recently deceased lobster into very large pot of salted, boiling water and cook for 15 minutes or until lobster is bright red. Serve.

Side Dish: Wild Rice

- **1   cup wild rice**
- **3³/4   cups water**
- **1/2   tsp. salt**

In cold water, rinse rice in wire strainer. Bring water and salt to a boil in saucepan. Add rice, stir and bring to a boil. Lower heat and simmer for 50 minutes or until rice is tender. Fluff rice with fork and simmer (uncovered) for 5 more minutes. Drain excess water and serve.

Side Dish: Green Beans

1   **lb. green beans**
2   **cups water**
1   **garlic clove, mashed**
    salt and pepper to taste
3   **T. butter**

Clean and cut green beans into 3-inch-long pieces. In saucepan, bring water to a boil and add beans and garlic. Cover and cook for 10 minutes or until tender; drain. Season with salt and pepper and serve with melted butter.

Dessert: Peach Melba

4-6   **fresh poached or canned peach halves**
      French vanilla or peach ice cream

Raspberry Sauce:
1   **cup fresh or frozen raspberries**
1   **T. sugar**
2   **T. Grand Marnier**
1   **tsp. lemon or lime juice**

In food processor or blender, puree raspberries with sugar. Stir in Grand Marnier and lemon or lime juice. Chill for 30 minutes.

In serving dishes, top each peach half with scoop of ice cream. Spoon on raspberry sauce. Serve immediately. (Note: Fresh peaches poached in 50-50 mix of good white wine and water until tender makes this dish sing like Melba!)

Italian Quick And Easy
Serves: 4-6

Italians migrated to the East Coast in huge numbers. Italian neighborhoods in New York and Boston still offer the flavor and taste of the old country. This easy menu relies on smoked fish, a tradition in both the Italian and Northern European cuisines. The following Northern Italian entree assembles and cooks in the same amount of time as pasta. The salad, cheese ball and desert can be made in advance for a rich, yet cooling menu that is ideal during summer or mild fall weather. If you do not smoke your own fish, try commercially smoked salmon or shad.

Appetizer: Smoked Fish Cheese Ball

1	**cup smoked fish**
8	**oz. cream cheese**
2	**tsp. grated onion**
1	**T. lemon juice**
1	**T. Worcestershire sauce**
4	**T. chopped parsley or walnuts**

Skin, bone and flake fish. Soften cream cheese and add fish, onion, lemon juice and Worcestershire sauce; blend well. Shape into ball or log and roll in parsley/ walnuts. Chill for 3-4 hours. Serve with quality crackers.

Salad: Butter Lettuce With Walnut Vinaigrette

1	**head butter-leaf lettuce**
2	**T. prepared Dijon-style mustard**
3	**T. red wine vinegar**
1/2	**cup olive oil**
1/2	**cup walnut pieces**
1	**T. parsley**
	salt and pepper

Rinse and tear lettuce leaves into bite-sized pieces; refrigerate. Combine mustard and vinegar in food processor or blender. Slowly add oil and beat until thoroughly mixed. Then add walnuts and parsley and continue to beat until finely chopped. Refrigerate and serve over salad. Dressing may be made in advance and added to lettuce just before serving.

Entree: Spinach Pasta With Smoked Fish And Cream Sauce

1 **cup flaked smoked fish (salmon)**
1 **lb. spinach pasta**
2 **cups heavy cream**
3 **T. butter**
1 **tsp. salt**
1 **T. ground pepper**
3 **T. grated Parmesan cheese**
1/3 **cup fresh dill, chopped**

Bring 4 quarts water to a boil in large pot. Add pasta and cook according to package directions or until done, yet slightly chewy. Meanwhile, combine cream and half of butter in saucepan and simmer over low heat. Add salt and pepper and continue cooking until cream is reduced by about one third. Add Parmesan cheese, smoked fish and fresh dill to cream mixture. Cook for 2-3 minutes over low heat. Drain pasta and toss with remaining butter. Stir in cream sauce and serve immediately with Parmesan cheese.

Dessert: Fresh Fruit Torte

This delicious dessert suits mild summer evenings on the porch. Use your favorite berries, sliced tree-ripened peaches or other fruit instead of traditional strawberries.

Cookie:
1 **stick butter, softened**
1/4 **cup sugar**
1/2 **cup almonds, finely chopped**
1 1/4 **cups flour**

Filling:
2 **cups berries or sliced fresh fruit**
  amaretto (optional)
2 **cups whipping cream**
3 **T. confectioners' sugar**
1 **tsp. almond extract**

Cookie can be made in advance: Cream butter and sugar in mixer bowl until light and fluffy. Add nuts and flour and beat until just blended. Lightly butter 2 large cookie sheets. Pat or roll dough into 4 or more circles ($^1/_4$ inch thick), depending on number of guests. Refrigerate dough for 15 minutes. Bake cookies at 375 degrees until golden brown (about 10-12 minutes). Let cool.

To make filling, slice berries or fruit in bowl. Add amaretto and refrigerate for 30 minutes. Whip cream until slightly thickened. Add sugar and almond extract to cream and continue whipping until stiff. When ready to serve, top cookie with cream, then fruit.

Veddy Proper British
Serves: 4-6

The strong, traditional British foods of the East Coast deserve a special menu. Striped bass on toast "crouttes" is exceptional. The warm spinach salad with bacon and lemon syllabub is totally delicious, and the following side dishes appear on many buffet tables. (With a baked potato, these side dishes can complete a meal for grilled bass.) The entire menu can be made quickly. Just start the syllabub early so it has time to set and separate before serving.

Appetizer: Sauteed Garlic Mushrooms

- **1   lb. fresh small whole mushrooms**
- **4   T. butter**
- **2   garlic cloves, minced**
- **2   T. fresh chopped parsley**
-      **salt and pepper to taste**

In skillet over low heat, melt butter and saute garlic until tender. Add mushrooms, toss and cook over medium heat until tender (about 5 minutes). Add parsley and salt and pepper. Toss and serve.

Salad: Hot Spinach And Bacon Salad

- **1   bunch fresh spinach**
- **6   bacon strips**

¹/₂ cup toasted sesame seeds
2 hard-cooked eggs, finely chopped

Dressing:
 3 T. red wine vinegar
¹/₂ tsp. sugar
 1 tsp. Dijon mustard

Rinse and drain spinach leaves, remove stems and break into bite-sized pieces. In small bowl, combine vinegar, sugar and mustard to make dressing; set aside. In skillet, cook bacon until crisp over medium heat. Remove bacon with slotted spoon and drain on paper towels. Crumble bacon in small bowl (reserve 2 T. bacon drippings); set aside. Add half of spinach to bacon drippings. Cook mixture for about 30 seconds. Add remaining spinach and toss gently for another 30 seconds. Remove from heat and add vinegar dressing and sesame seeds; toss lightly. Divide salad portions onto salad plates and sprinkle hard-cooked eggs and crumbled bacon over top.

Entree: Striped Bass On Buttered Crouttes

2¹/₂ lbs. striper steaks, sliced 2 inches thick
 ¹/₂ cup olive oil
 1 onion, sliced
 1 green pepper, sliced
 3 garlic cloves, minced
 1 cup dry red wine
 1 T. fresh chopped parsley
 ¹/₄ tsp. salt
 ¹/₄ tsp. pepper
 ¹/₈ tsp. paprika
 3 medium tomatoes, sliced
 4-6 bread slices, 1/2 inch thick
 4 T. butter
 1 tsp. garlic powder

In skillet, add ¹/₄ cup oil over medium heat. Add onion, green pepper and garlic and cook until tender (about 5 minutes). Pour in wine and add parsley, salt, pepper and paprika; bring to a boil. Add striped bass, cover and cook for 30 minutes or until fish flakes when tested with fork. Remove bass to warm platter and keep warm. Boil sauce over high heat until thickened (about 5 minutes), stirring frequently.

In separate skillet, melt butter with remaining oil over medium heat. Add garlic powder. Fry bread slices on both sides until golden brown. Remove bread to platter. Place striped bass on top of bread slices. Add tomato slices and pour sauce over all.

Dessert: Lemon Syllabub

2	egg whites
1/2	cup powder sugar
	rind from 1 lemon, finely grated
1 1/2	T. lemon juice
1 1/4	cup heavy cream
2/3	cup dry white wine
	lemon slices

In electric mixer, whisk egg whites until peaks form. Fold in sugar, lemon rind and lemon juice. Whip cream with wine until thick and floppy. Fold cream into egg-white mixture and divide into serving glasses. Place in refrigerator for 4-5 hours to separate slightly. Decorate with lemon slices and serve with your favorite cookie. (This English custard represents an entire class of syllabubs. You can use grated orange and orange juice, berry and berry juice combinations, port, sherry and other "additives." All will separate slightly when they set. The lighter texture of the frothy top contrasts nicely with the more solid lower section. Easy, inexpensive, light and delicious. Who could ask for more?)

Simply Shad!
Serves: 2-4

Because shad come in huge numbers, here's a complete shad meal (except, of course, the dessert) for shad addicts. It's dandy when the runs peak, your smoker's full and you can't give away fish. Broiled shad, however, require cleaning.

Appetizer: Shad Cakes

- **6** cups cooked shad, shredded and boned
- **2** cups water-soaked bread
- **2** eggs, separated
- **1** T. dried parsley flakes
- **2** T. Parmesan cheese
- **2** T. lemon juice
- **1/4** tsp. salt
- **1/8** tsp. pepper
- **2** T. oil

Hollandaise-Tarragon Sauce:
- **1** stick plus 2 T. butter
- **3** egg yolks
  pinch of salt
- **2** T. lemon juice
- **2** T. half-and-half or heavy cream
- **1/4** tsp. tarragon leaves

Cut day-old French bread into large pieces, cover with water and soak for 10 minutes. Remove bread, discard crust and squeeze out excess water; crumble. Add shad, egg yolks, parsley, cheese, lemon juice, salt and pepper. Mix well. Lightly brush oil onto cookie sheet. Shape shad mixture into 2-inch patties or golf-sized balls and place on pan. Bake for 25 minutes or until brown at 350 degrees.

To make hollandaise-tarragon sauce, melt butter over low heat. In blender, beat egg yolks and salt for 30 seconds. Slowly pour in half of butter while blending at medium speed. Blend until thickened. Reduce speed; add lemon juice and remaining butter. Increase speed to medium-high and add half-and-half and tarragon. Blend for 30 seconds. Serve sauce over patties or as dip for balls.

Salad: Roe Salad Maryland

- **1/2** lb. fresh shad roe (see recipe below)
- **1** T. prepared horseradish
- **3/4** cup mayonnaise
- **1/8** tsp. thyme

2   **celery stalks, chopped**
8   **stuffed green olives, chopped**
1/2   **cucumber, diced**
1/4   **tsp. salt**
1/8   **tsp. pepper**
1/2   **head lettuce**

Place roe in boiling water and simmer for 15 minutes; drain. Cool roe at room temperature and cut into cubes; set aside. Blend horseradish, mayonnaise and thyme. In large bowl, combine celery, olives, cucumber, salt and pepper. Add horseradish dressing and mix well. Gently stir in roe cubes. Line chilled salad plates with lettuce and top with roe mixture. Serve cold.

Basic Roe Preparation:
1   **shad roe**
1/4   **tsp. salt (optional)**
1   **T. white vinegar or lemon juice**
4   **cups water**

Clean roe. Add salt and vinegar to water; bring to a boil. Add roe and cook for 20 minutes; drain and cover with cold water for 3 minutes. Remove membrane. Chill before preparing recipes.

Entree: Broiled Shad

1   **lb. shad fillets**
1/4   **cup melted butter or margarine**
2   **T. lemon juice**
1/4   **tsp. Worcestershire sauce**
1/4   **tsp. dried thyme leaves**
1/4   **tsp. dried basil leaves**
1/8   **tsp. salt**
1/8   **tsp. pepper**

Scale and fillet shad. Combine butter, lemon juice, Worcestershire sauce, thyme, basil, salt and pepper. Place shad skin-side up in broiler pan. Brush butter mixture over fillets. Broil 6 inches from top of broiler for 7 minutes. Turn carefully and brush remaining butter mixture over fillets. Broil for 5 more minutes or until fish flakes when tested with fork. (Note: A shad scales easily immediately after it is caught.)

Dessert: Red Chocolate Cake

2	cups flour	**Frosting:**	
3	T. cocoa	1	cup milk
1	tsp. salt	1/4	cup flour
1/2	cup shortening		salt
11/2	cups sugar	1	cup sugar
2	eggs	1/2	cup shortening
1	oz. red food coloring	1/2	cup butter or
1	tsp. vanilla		margarine
1	cup buttermilk	1	tsp. vanilla
1	T. vinegar		
1	tsp. baking soda		

Preheat oven to 350 degrees. Grease and flour two 9-inch round cake pans. Sift flour, cocoa and salt. In separate bowl, cream shortening with sugar. Add eggs, red food coloring and vanilla. Mix well. Beat while gradually adding flour mix and buttermilk to eggs. Mix vinegar and baking soda separately; fold into batter. Pour batter into prepared pans and bake for 30 minutes.

To make frosting, heat milk and flour over medium-high heat, stirring until thick. Add pinch of salt and cool. Beat sugar with remaining ingredients until fluffy. Add flour mix and beat everything until well-blended. Frost cooled cake and refrigerate until ready to serve.

German Pike & Other Delights
Serves: 4

German mercenary soldiers lured away from King George's army by the promise of land and money in Philadelphia became the Pennsylvania Dutch. Solid, hearty menus appropriate for those who worked the land resulted. Baked fish with caper sauce, or Gebackener Fisch mit Kapernsauce, goes nicely with a filling side dish called "Heaven and Earth," a light German mushroom salad and a bread pudding made with rye bread. Eggs stuffed with crab meat make a great appetizer for this wonderful meal.

Appetizer: Eggs Stuffed With Crab Meat

6 hard-cooked eggs, peeled
3/4 cup crab meat, flaked
2 celery stalks, finely chopped
1 tsp. dry mustard
1/3 cup mayonnaise
1/2 tsp. onion powder
    salt and pepper to taste
    paprika for garnish

Cut cooked eggs in half lengthwise. Scoop out yolks and mash them in small bowl. Combine crab meat, celery, mustard, mayonnaise and onion powder. Season mixture with salt and pepper. Heap egg whites into mixture. Top with paprika and chill until needed.

Salad: German Mushroom Salad

1 lb. fresh mushrooms, sliced
4 sweet pickles, finely diced
2 T. minced onion (red if possible)
1 garlic clove, minced
1 tomato, seeded and finely chopped
1/2 cup salad oil
1/2 cup malt, red wine or plain vinegar
1 tsp. sugar
I head lettuce, separated into 6 sections

Combine mushrooms, pickles, onion, garlic clove and tomato; toss. Add oil, vinegar and sugar. Separate lettuce into 6 sections, forming "cups" to hold ingredients. Put ingredients into lettuce cups. Chill for 2-3 hours.

Entree: Pike—Or The Like—With Caper Sauce

1 3-lb. whole pike
1/2 tsp. salt
1/2 cup melted butter
4 T. flour
2 cups hot fish stock or chicken bouillon
3 tsp. capers

4   anchovy fillets, minced
1/2   tsp. sugar
3   T. lemon juice

Heat oven to 350 degrees. Clean fish and rinse. Season inside with salt. Put fish in buttered baking dish and top with melted butter. Cook for 25 minutes or until fish flakes when tested with fork. Remove fish from oven, place on plate or platter, cover and keep warm. Stir flour into fish juices over moderate heat. Add stock gradually. Cook until thickened. Then stir in capers, anchovies, sugar and lemon juice. Serve with or over fish.

Side Dish: Heaven & Earth

1/2   lb. bacon, diced
      oil
2   large onions, sliced
1   tsp. lemon rind
2 1/2   cups applesauce (chunky homemade
      or 28-oz. jar
2   cups mashed hot potatoes (not instant!)
      salt and pepper to taste

In large skillet, fry bacon in oil. Add onions and cook until golden brown. Mix lemon rind, applesauce and hot potatoes just before onions brown. Stir all ingredients together and season with salt and pepper.

Dessert: Bread Pudding

10   day-old bread slices (rye), cut into cubes
1 1/2   cup apple cider or apple jack
      butter
1/2   cup sugar
1 1/2   tsp. cinnamon
2   lbs. apples, cored, peeled and sliced
1/2   cup yellow or dark raisins
3   T. butter or margarine

Heat oven to 350 degrees. Mix bread cubes and cider to soften. Butter 2-qt. casserole. Combine sugar and cinnamon (if apples are extremely tart, add more sugar). Alternately layer bread, apple slices, sugar/cinnamon, ending with bread layer. Dot top with butter. Sprinkle sugar over top and bake for 45 minutes. Serve with ice cream or whipped cream.

The Great Chowder Controversy
Serves: 6-8

Boston or Manhattan? White or red? Potatoes or tomatoes? Arguments rage in the East. So here is a double-chowder entree menu, with a shad hor d'oeuvre and a simple rhubarb and orange crumble. Serve both chowders (you can substitute or supplement clams with fish if you like). Add French bread hot from the oven and let your guests argue. (Bonus: All you need do at the last minute is take the French bread out of the oven and slap ice cream or whipped cream on the dessert before it's served.)

Appetizer: Shad Roe With Toast

1	shad roe (see Basic Roe Preparation recipe)
4	T. butter
2	T. lemon juice
2	hard-cooked egg yolks, mashed
1	T. bread crumbs
1	tsp. parsley flakes
1/8	tsp. salt
1/8	tsp. pepper
	toast strips or triangles

Cook roe according to Basic Roe Preparation recipe (on page 56). After roe has chilled, break up lightly with fork. In skillet, melt butter with lemon juice over medium heat. Add roe, mashed egg yolks, bread crumbs, parsley, salt and pepper. Stir until well blended. Serve hot over toast strips.

Entree No.1: Boston Clam Chowder

3	T. butter or margarine
1	2-inch cube salt pork
1	medium onion, chopped
2	7¹/₂-oz cans clams, minced or chopped

1   **cup water**
3   **medium potatoes, diced into 1/2-inch cubes**
1   **cup milk**
1¹/₂   **cups heavy cream**
¹/₈   **tsp. white pepper**

Dice salt pork into ¹/₄-inch cubes. Melt butter in saucepan over medium heat. Saute salt pork and chopped onion until brown. Strain clam juice into saucepan and reserve clams. Add water and potatoes and cook until potatoes are tender. Heat milk and cream in separate pan. Do not boil. Add reserved clams, pepper and warmed milk to potato mixture and simmer for 3 minutes. Serve immediately.

Entree No. 2: Manhattan Clam Chowder

¹/₄   **lb. salt pork**
1   **medium onion, chopped**
3   **T. flour**
1   **8-oz. bottle clam juice**
1¹/₂   **cups water or fish stock**
3   **medium potatoes, diced into ¹/₂-inch cubes**
5   **medium tomatoes or 3 cups canned stewed tomatoes, chopped**
1   **tsp. thyme leaves**
1   **bay leaf**
1   **tsp. parsley flakes**
3   **7¹/₂-oz cans clams, chopped or minced pepper**

Dice salt pork into ¹/₄-inch cubes and brown over medium heat. Add onions and saute until tender. Stir in flour and slowly pour in clam juice, water or stock and boil. Add potatoes, tomatoes, thyme, bay leaf and parsley. Reduce heat, cover and simmer for 15 minutes or until potatoes are tender. Add chopped clams and simmer for 5 more minutes. Discard bay leaf, add pepper to taste and serve.

Dessert: Rhubarb And Orange Crumble

1¹/₂   lbs. rhubarb (strawberries can substitute)
**   4   T. sugar**
**   rind from 1 orange, grated**
**   juice from ¹/₂ orange**
**   whipped cream or ice cream**

Topping:
**   1   cup flour**
**   1   tsp. baking powder**
** ³/₄ cup sugar**
** ¹/₂ cup chopped almonds**
**   1   stick butter**

Wash and trim rhubarb, discarding woody ends and all leaves. Cut rhubarb into ¹/₂-inch pieces. In bowl, combine rhubarb, sugar, orange rind and orange juice. In 9x13-inch baking pan, spread rhubarb mixture out evenly. To make topping, sift flour and baking powder together. Add sugar and almonds; mix well. Rub butter into flour until mixture resembles bread crumbs, then spread over rhubarb mixture. Bake at 350 degrees for 40 minutes or until crumble is golden and crisp. Serve warm or cold with whip cream or ice cream. (Rhubarb leaves are poisonous, so you must remove them if you grow your own rhubarb.)

Recipes For:

Crappie

Croaker

Crustaceans

Flounder

Froglegs

Grouper

Grunion

Haddock

Special Fried Crappie

Serves: 4-6
Prep Time: 30-45 minutes

 **3 lbs. crappie fillets
   vegetable oil or shortening
 2 cups self-rising cornmeal
 2 T. all-purpose flour
   black pepper to taste
 4 eggs beaten**

In large skillet or deep-fat fryer, heat oil to 360 degrees.
Combine cornmeal, flour and pepper in shallow bowl. Beat
eggs in separate shallow bowl. Dry fillets with paper towels.
Alternate dredging fillets in egg mixture then cornmeal mixture
until fillets are coated with batter. Set coated fillets aside for a
few minutes then fry until golden brown. Cut fillets into bite-
sized pieces and serve with lemon wedges or Jack's Red
Dipping Sauce (see recipe below).

Jack's Red Dipping Sauce

Serves: several (yields 2 cups)
Prep Time: 20-30 minutes

 **1 1/2 cups catsup
  2 T. brown sugar
  2 T. Worcestershire sauce
  1 tsp. dry mustard
 1/3 cup Jack Daniel's Tennessee whiskey**

In small saucepan, combine all ingredients, except whiskey.
Bring to a boil, stirring occasionally. Stir in whiskey and simmer
for 5 minutes. Refrigerate before serving. Serve with fried or
steamed crappies.

Steamed Crappies

Serves: 8
Prep Time: 45 minutes

**3   lbs. crappie fillets
salt and pepper to taste**

Rinse fillets and dry with paper towels. Season fillets with salt and pepper. Place fillets in single layer on heavy aluminum foil. Form packet by folding over ends of foil, sealing securely. Place fillets on baking sheet and bake for 10-15 minutes. Serve fish warm or with Jack's Red Dipping Sauce.

Fried Fish

Serves: 1-2
Prep Time: 20 minutes

**2   lbs. crappie fillets
1/2   cup dry onion-ring mix
cooking oil**

Rinse fish fillets and put into plastic bag with onion-ring mix. In cast-iron skillet, heat oil and fry fillets until fish flakes.

Thomas Schaad
Leawood, Kansas

Wine-Spiced Croaker

Serves: 2-4
Prep Time: 1 hour, 15 minutes

4	croakers, dressed
1/4	cup lime juice
1/2	cup white wine
1/2	cup sherry
1/4	tsp. nutmeg
1/8	tsp. ginger
1/4	tsp. salt
1/8	tsp. pepper
1	stick butter
2	T. lemon peel, grated
2	T. parsley
1	cup red grapes (seedless)
1/2	cup toasted almonds, sliced

Combine lime juice, wine, sherry, nutmeg and ginger. Make three small diagonal incisions on each side of each croaker. Season fish with salt and pepper inside and out. Marinate in wine mixture for 1 hour, turning several times. Remove fish, dry between paper towels and reserve marinade. In skillet, melt butter and saute fish for 5-7 minutes or until fish is tender and flakes easily when tested with fork. Place fish on warm platter, add marinade to skillet and simmer. Add lemon peel, parsley and grapes to marinade; pour marinade over fish. Sprinkle toasted almond over top and serve.

Easy Pan-Fried Croaker

Serves: 6
Prep Time: 20-30 minutes

6	**croakers, dressed**
1	**cup cornmeal**
1	**tsp. paprika**
1/2	**tsp. celery salt**
1/4	**tsp. garlic powder**
1/2	**tsp. celery seed**
1/2	**tsp. lemon-pepper seasoning**
1/2	**tsp. dry mustard**
1	**tsp. instant onion, minced**
1	**cup milk**
	cooking oil

Wash fish and pat dry. Combine cornmeal and seasonings. Dip fish in milk and roll in seasoned cornmeal. In large skillet, heat oil. Fry 3 fish at a time on medium heat for 4-5 minutes or until lightly browned. Turn carefully; fry an additional 4-5 minutes or until fish are brown and flaky. Repeat process with remaining fish. Drain on paper towels and garnish with lemon wedges and red pepper strips.

Champion Shrimp

Serves: 6
Prep Time: 30 minutes

3	**lbs. medium-sized shrimp, unshelled**
1/2	**lb. butter or margarine**
1/2	**tsp. garlic powder**
	pepper to taste

Put unshelled shrimp into oblong baking pan. (If you remove the shell, the flavor is cut in half!) Add butter and garlic powder; sprinkle pepper over shrimp generously. Turn shrimp occasionally. Shrimp are done when pink. Serve with sauce and chunks of Italian or French bread. Guests may remove shells from shrimp and dunk bread and shrimp directly in sauce.

John O'Toole
Alamo, Texas

Hot Lobster Ring

Serves: 5
Prep Time: 40-50 minutes

2	**cups cooked lobster meat, diced**	**1/2**	**cup bread crumbs**
2	**T. butter**	**4**	**egg yolks, beaten**
3	**T. flour**	**1/2**	**tsp. salt**
2	**cups chicken bouillon**	**1/4**	**tsp. pepper**
1	**T. parsley, minced**	**4**	**egg whites**

In saucepan, melt butter and add flour, stirring until blended. Gradually stir in bouillon. Add parsley, bread crumbs, yolks, lobster, salt and pepper. Remove from heat. In separate bowl, whip egg whites until stiff. Fold egg white into lobster mixture and place mixture in well-oiled 9-inch ring mold. Bake at 325 degrees for 20 minutes or until firm. Unmold and serve.

Maine Lobster Quiche

Serves: several
Prep Time: 1 hour, 50 minutes

1¹/₂	cups fresh lobster, chopped	1	8-inch baked pie shell
3	oz. Swiss cheese, shredded	2	eggs
3	oz. Gruyere cheese, shredded	1	cup light cream
1	T. flour	2	T. sherry
		¹/₂	tsp. salt
		¹/₄	tsp. pepper
			dash paprika

Sprinkle lobster, cheeses and flour over bottom of pie shell. Beat eggs. Combine eggs, cream, sherry, salt and pepper. Pour egg mixture over in pie shell. Place pie shell on cookie sheet and bake at 350 degrees for 45-60 minutes or until set. Cool slightly for 15 minutes before cutting.

Micro-Easy Lobster Newburg

Serves: 4
Prep Time: 20-40 minutes

2	cups cooked lobster meat, diced	3	egg yolks, lightly beaten
2	T. butter	¹/₂	tsp. salt
¹/₄	cup dry sherry	¹/₄	tsp. pepper
¹/₂	tsp. paprika	1	cup cream

In deep 3-qt. casserole, melt butter and add sherry; microwave on high for 2 minutes. Add paprika, egg yolks, salt and pepper and blend with wire whisk. Microwave on high for 45 seconds. Whisk in cream and add cooked lobster meat. Microwave an additional 1-2 minutes on medium or until mixture is hot. (Do not boil.) Serve over toast or hot rice.

Savory Deviled Crab

Serves: 4
Prep Time: 45-60 minutes

1¹/₂	cups cooked crab meat
3	T. butter
¹/₄	cup onion, chopped
¹/₄	cup green peppers, chopped
¹/₄	cup celery, chopped
¹/₄	cup cracker crumbs
³/₄	cup milk
2	eggs, beaten
¹/₄	tsp. salt
1¹/₂	tsp. mustard
	dash paprika
4	crab shells

In large saucepan or skillet, melt 2 T. butter and saute onion, green pepper and celery until tender. Add cracker crumbs and milk; cook until mixture is thick. Remove from heat and add eggs, salt, mustard, paprika and crab meat. Pack this mixture into crab shells (individual baking dishes can be used). Brush tops with 1 T. melted butter and bake at 400 degrees or broil until brown.

Classic Crab Louis

Serves: 4
Prep Time: 30-45 minutes

2	**cups cooked crab meat**
3/4	**cup lettuce, shredded**
1	**cup mayonnaise**
1/4	**cup heavy cream**
1/4	**cup prepared mild salsa**
1	**tsp. Worcestershire sauce**
1/4	**cup green pepper, chopped**
1/4	**cup green onion, chopped**
2	**T. lemon juice**
1/2	**tsp. salt**
	hard-boiled eggs, sliced
	cherry tomatoes, halved
	avocado chunks
	chives

Divide lettuce among 4 serving dishes and heat 1/2 cup crab meat on each. Combine mayonnaise, cream, salsa, Worcestershire sauce, green pepper, onion, lemon juice and salt. Pour pour mixture over crab meat. Garnish with hard-boiled eggs, cherry tomatoes, avocado chunks and chives.

Sharon's Hot Crab Dip

Serves: several
Prep Time: 25-40 minutes

2	cups cooked crab meat, shredded
8	oz. cream cheese
1	T. milk
2	tsp. onion, finely chopped
1/2	tsp. horseradish
1/4	tsp. salt
	dash pepper
1/3	cup toasted almonds, sliced

Combine all ingredients, except almonds, in ovenproof dish; blend well. Top with almonds and bake at 375 degrees for 15 minutes.

Fluffy King Crab Omelet

Serves: 2
Prep Time: 20-30 minutes

6	oz. king crab meat, diced or shredded (3-4 legs)
5	eggs, separated
2	T. water
1/4	tsp. baking powder
2	T. butter
4	T. prepared Creole sauce

Beat egg whites until they form peaks. Combine egg yolks, water and baking powder. Gently fold mixture into beaten egg whites. In omelet pan, melt butter and add eggs. Cook over low heat until bottom is golden. Place pan in oven and bake at 350 degrees for 10 minutes or until omelet is set and fluffy. Spoon Creole sauce and crab meat into center of omelet, fold and serve.

King Crab Jambalaya

Serves: 6-8
Prep Time: 20-30 minutes

2	cups king crab meat, diced or shredded
1	T. butter
1/4	cup onion, chopped
1	T. flour
1	cup tomatoes, diced
1/3	cup water
3	cups cooked rice
1/4	tsp. dried thyme
2	T. parsley, chopped
1/2	cup shredded cheddar cheese

In large saucepan, melt butter and saute onion until limp and golden. Stir in flour and add tomatoes and water. Bring mixture to a boil and reduce heat. Stir in rice, crab and thyme. Cook over low heat for 10 minutes, stirring frequently. Sprinkle parsley and cheese over top before serving.

Crab-A-Rama With Sauces

Serves: several
Prep Time: 30-45 minutes

>   king crab legs
>   crab meat
>   shrimp
>   scallops
>   oysters
>   mussels or any other shellfish
>   Romaine lettuce leaves

Cucumber Sauce:
- 1   cup sour cream
- 1   T. fresh chives, minced
- 1   medium cucumber, unpeeled and finely chopped
- 1   T. white wine vinegar

Mustard Sauce:
- 1/2   cup oil
- 2   T. sugar
- 1/2   cup white wine vinegar
- 4   T. Dijon mustard
-     dash white pepper

Prepare shellfish of your choice on large platter lined with individual romaine lettuce leaves (use crushed ice on platter to keep fish cool). To make cucumber sauce, mix cucumber-sauce ingredients in blender or food processor and chill. To make mustard sauce, mix all mustard-sauce ingredients in blender or food processor and chill. Serve sauces with cold shellfish.

Crayfish Kabobs

Serves: 4
Prep Time: 40-55 minutes

1	lb. crayfish, shelled	1/2	lb. whole mushrooms
2	T. oil	1	can pineapple chunks
1	T. lemon juice	2	green peppers, cut
1/4	tsp. paprika		into squares
1/4	tsp. garlic powder	1/2	lb. small onions

Combine oil, lemon juice, paprika and garlic powder to form marinade. Marinate crayfish in mixture for 30 minutes. Arrange crayfish on skewers alternately with mushrooms, pineapple chunks, green pepper squares and onions. Broil 3 inches from heat for 5-7 minutes on each side, basting occasionally with left-over marinade.

Crayfish With Peppers

Serves: 6
Prep Time: 25-40 minutes

1 1/2	lbs. crayfish, shelled	2	tsp. dried basil
2	T. lemon juice	1	T. cooking oil
3	garlic cloves, minced	1/2	cup red bell pepper,
1/2	tsp. black pepper		diced
1	T. olive oil	1/2	cup green bell pepper,
2	tsp. dried oregano		diced
2	T. parsley, chopped		

In small bowl, combine lemon juice, garlic, pepper, oil, oregano, parsley and basil. Add crayfish and marinate for 15 minutes. Heat oil in wok or large skillet and saute green and red bell peppers until slightly tender. Add crayfish and marinade; saute for 2-3 minutes. Serve over bed of hot rice.

Micro-Easy Alhambra Creole

Serves: 4-6
Prep Time: 20-30 minutes

36	crayfish, shelled and cooked	1/2	cup green pepper, chopped
1	16-oz. can stewed tomatoes	1	tsp. sugar
1	tsp. garlic powder		dash hot sauce (optional)
1/2	cup onion, chopped		salt and pepper to taste

Combine all ingredients, except crayfish, in deep 3-qt. casserole. Cover and microwave on high for 6-8 minutes. Add precooked and shelled crayfish; stir well. Microwave on high for 4-5 minutes or until heated thoroughly. Serve over hot, cooked rice.

Micro-Easy Quick Shrimp Soup

Serves: 4
Prep Time: 25-40 minutes

- 1/2 lb. fresh shrimp
- 1 can cream of shrimp soup
- 1 1/2 cups milk
- 1 10-oz. pkg. mixed vegetables in cream sauce
- 2 T. dry sherry
- 1/4 tsp. dried dillweed
- 2 T. Parmesan cheese, grated

In 2-qt casserole, combine soup and milk; stir until smooth. Add frozen vegetables with sauce, sherry and dillweed. Cover and microwave on high for 6 minutes. Stir well until sauce is creamy. Add shrimp and cover. Microwave on high for 10 minutes until thoroughly heated, stirring once. Stir in Parmesan cheese. Cover and let stand for 2 minutes. Stir before serving.

Shrimp New Orleans Style

Serves: several
Prep Time: 12 hours, 30-40 minutes

2	lbs. medium shrimp, simmered, peeled and deveined
1	large garlic clove, split
6	T. olive oil
3	T. lemon juice
5	T. horseradish
2	T. prepared mustard
	lettuce leaves, shredded
1	T. chives, finely chopped
1	green onion, finely chopped
1/2	tsp. white pepper
1/2	tsp. salt (optional)
1/4	tsp. paprika
1/4	tsp. hot pepper sauce

Rub inside of bowl with garlic. In bowl, combine all ingredients except shrimp and lettuce. Add shrimp and stir carefully to coat. Cover and marinate in refrigerator for up to 12 hours. When ready to serve, remove shrimp from refrigerator and place on bed of lettuce.

Shrimp In Garlic Butter

Serves: 6
Prep Time: 20-30 minutes

2	**lbs. fresh shrimp**
8	**T. unsalted butter**
1/2	**cup olive oil**
1	**T. lemon juice**
1/4	**cup shallots or green onions, finely chopped**
1	**T. garlic, finely chopped**
1	**tsp. salt**
	dash black pepper
4	**T. fresh parsley, finely chopped**
1	**lemon, cut into 6 wedges**

Preheat broiler to highest temperature. In large, shallow oven-proof baking dish, melt butter over low heat (do not brown). Stir in olive oil, lemon juice, shallots, garlic, salt and pepper. Add shrimp and stir in mixture until coated. Broil 3-4 inches from heat for 5 minutes; turn over and broil another 5-10 minutes until lightly browned and firm to touch. Do not overcook. Transfer shrimp to warm serving platter. Pour sauce on shrimp from pan and sprinkle parsley over top. Garnish with lemon wedges.

Flounder Chowder

Serves: several
Prep Time: 1 hour, 30-45 minutes

1 **lb. flounder chunks**
4 **cups milk**
1 **lb. pkg. frozen mixed vegetables**
2 **potatoes, diced**
2 **T. butter**
1/4 **tsp. pepper**

Place fish in roasting pan almost filled with milk. Cover and bake at 350 degrees for 1 hour or until fish is almost done. Add frozen vegetables, potatoes and butter. Lower heat to 250 degrees and cook for 20 minutes or until vegetables are tender. Sprinkle pepper over fish. Serve with chowder crackers.

Oven-Fried Flounder

Serves: 4
Prep Time: 20-30 minutes

4 **large flounder fillets**
1/2 **cup milk**
1/2 **tsp. salt**
1/2 **cup dried bread crumbs**
3 **T. melted butter**

Combine milk and salt in shallow pan; dip fillets into milk. Coat fillets with bread crumbs and place fish in well-oiled baking dish. Pour melted butter over fillets and bake at 350 degrees for 10-12 minutes or until tender and flaky.

Foiled Flounder and Veggie Bake

Serves: 4
Prep Time: 25-35 minutes

4	**large flounder fillets**
1-2	**medium potatoes, peeled and sliced**
1	**carrot, julienned**
1/4	**lb. fresh green beans (whole)**
1	**medium onion, sliced**
3	**T. margarine**
2	**tsp. basil**
	salt and pepper to taste

Place each fish fillet on 12-inch piece of aluminum foil. On each fillet place 1/4 of potatoes, carrot, green beans and onion. Dot each fillet with margarine and sprinkle with 1/2 tsp. basil. Season with salt and pepper. Fold up edges of foil and seal packets. Place packets on cookie sheet and bake at 400 degrees for 10-15 minutes or until tender and flaky.

Micro-Easy Florentine Flounder

Serves: 4-6
Prep Time: 20-30 minutes

1-1¹/₂ lbs. flounder fillets (4-6 large fillets)
1   10-oz. pkg. frozen spinach or
1   cup fresh spinach, cooked
¹/₄   cup wheat germ
¹/₄   tsp. grated nutmeg
1   egg, slightly beaten
¹/₄   tsp. salt
¹/₄   tsp. pepper
2   T. Parmesan cheese
¹/₃   cup cooking oil
dash paprika
4-6   tomato slices
parsley sprigs

Combine defrosted spinach, wheat germ, nutmeg, egg, salt, pepper and cheese. Spread evenly over each fillet and roll up (jelly-roll style), securing ends with toothpicks. Place seam-side down in 7x12-inch buttered baking dish. Brush each fillet with oil, sprinkle with paprika and top with tomato slices. Cover and microwave on high for 5-7 minutes or until center of fish begins to flake when tested with fork. Let stand (covered) for 5 minutes. Garnish with parsley sprigs before serving.

Braised Froglegs

Serves: 4
Prep Time: 25-35 minutes

8	large froglegs	3/4	cup chicken bouillon
12	T. butter	1 1/4	cups bread crumbs
1/4	cup onions, chopped	1	tsp. lemon juice
1/4	cup flour		

In large skillet, melt 6 T. butter and saute onions until golden.
Roll froglegs in flour and add to skillet, browning on both sides.
Reduce heat and add bouillon. Cover skillet and cook for 10
minutes or until legs are tender. In separate pan, melt 6 T. butter
and saute bread crumbs. Stir in lemon juice. Roll froglegs in
bread-crumb mixture to coat. Serve.

Frog Bonne Femme

Serves: 3
Prep Time: 30-45 minutes

6	large froglegs	1	cup mushrooms, sliced
1 1/2	cups chicken bouillon		
1/2	cup white wine	1 1/2	T. flour
2	lemon slices	1/4	tsp. salt
1/8	tsp. pepper	3	egg yolks
3	T. butter	3	T. cream

Cut frogleg meat into 3-4 pieces. Place meat in saucepan and
cover with bouillon and wine. Add lemon slices and pepper.
Cover and simmer until meat is tender. Remove frog meat and
reserve 1 1/2 cups of liquid. In separate saucepan, melt butter
and saute mushrooms until light brown. Stir in flour and salt.
Gradually add reserved liquid. When sauce is hot, add frog
meat and reduce heat. Beat egg yolks and cream together, stirring into meat. Remove from heat and allow to thicken.

Ol' South Froglegs

Serves: 6
Prep Time: 1 hour, 30-40 minutes

12-18 froglegs
- **1   T. cornstarch**
- **1   T. lemon juice**
- **2   T. mayonnaise**
-     **dash salt and pepper**
- **2   eggs, beaten**
- **2/3   cup flour**
- **1/3   cup dry seasoned bread crumbs**
-     **oil**

Combine cornstarch, lemon juice, mayonnaise, salt and pepper and eggs; blend well. Place froglegs in heavy plastic bag or sealed container; pour mixture over legs. Seal and marinate in refrigerator for 1 hour. Combine flour and bread crumbs in separate plastic bag; add 2-3 legs at a time to flour mixture and shake to coat evenly. In heavy skillet, preheat oil 3 inches deep. Fry legs, a few at a time, for 2-3 minutes or until golden brown. Remove and drain on paper towels. Arrange on platter, garnish and keep warm before serving.

Broiled Breaded Grouper

Serves: 4
Prep Time: 15-20 minutes

1	lb. grouper, cut into serving-sized pieces
1¹/₂	T. butter, melted
¹/₄	cup dry bread crumbs
1	T. parsley, chopped
¹/₈	tsp. pepper
¹/₈	tsp. paprika

Coat grouper pieces on all sides with melted butter. Combine bread crumbs, parsley, pepper and paprika. Dip fish into bread crumb mixture and place on broiling pan. Broil for 10 minutes or until fish is flaky and tender.

Easy Grouper With Broccoli

Serves: 4
Prep Time: 20-30 minutes

1	lb. grouper fillets
1	medium onion, chopped
1	10-oz. pkg frozen broccoli, thawed and coarsely chopped
¹/₄	tsp. pepper
1	tsp. tarragon
1	T. butter
¹/₄	cup white wine

Combine onion and thawed broccoli; spread in 8-inch square baking dish. Place fillets over broccoli and season with pepper and tarragon. Dot with butter and pour wine over fish. Cover and bake at 400 degrees for 15-20 minutes or until fish is flaky and tender.

Micro-Easy Sunshine Grouper Bake

Serves: 6
Prep Time: 35-45 minutes

2	lbs. grouper fillets
1/2	cup celery, chopped
1/4	cup onion, chopped
2	T. orange rind, grated
1/4	cup butter or margarine
3/4	cup orange juice
3/4	cup water
2	T. lemon juice
1/2	tsp. salt
1 1/2	cups instant rice, uncooked
1	medium lemon, sliced
1	medium orange, sliced
	parsley sprigs

Combine celery, onion, orange rind and butter in large measuring cup or small bowl. Cover with waxed paper and microwave on high for 2 minutes. Stir in orange juice, water, lemon juice and salt. Cover with waxed paper and microwave on high for 7 minutes or until mixture boils. Remove from oven and stir in rice. Cover with waxed paper and let stand for 5 minutes. Spoon rice into lightly greased 12x8-inch baking dish. Place fillets on top of rice and cover with waxed paper. Microwave on high for 10-11 minutes, rotating dish every 3 minutes. Remove from oven and let stand (covered) for 5 minutes. Garnish with lemon and orange slices and parsley sprigs. Serve immediately.

Fried Grunion

Serves: 6
Prep Time: 20 minutes

	grunion, gutted
1	**cup flour**
1	**cup cornmeal**
1	**tsp. thyme**
2	**T. salt**
	cooking oil
2	**lemons, cut into wedges**

Gut and rinse grunion, retaining head and tail; set aside.
Combine flour, cornmeal, thyme and salt. Dredge fish in mixture
and deep-fry in preheated, oiled skillet. Fry until fish is golden
brown, turning once. Serve with lemon wedges.

John Gagliardo
Oxnard, California

Cajun Baked Haddock

Serves: 6
Prep Time: 25-35 minutes

1¹/₂ lbs. haddock fillets
¹/₂-³/₄ cajun seasoning mix
 ¹/₂ tsp. garlic powder
 ¹/₂ tsp. paprika
 ¹/₄ tsp. pepper
 2 T. cooking oil
 1 T. parsley, chopped

Combine cajun seasoning mix, garlic powder, paprika and pepper in shallow dish. Spread cooking oil over fillets and roll fish in spices to coat evenly. Place fish in baking dish and bake at 450 degrees for 10 minutes per inch of thickness or until fish is flaky and tender. Sprinkle parsley over top before serving.

Haddock Orange Onion Bake

Serves: 2
Prep Time: 20-30 minutes

¹/₂ lb. haddock fillets   **¹/₂ onion, sliced**
¹/₄ tsp. pepper   **1 orange, peeled and**
 1 T. lemon juice   **sliced**
 1 T. cooking oil   **2 T. parsley, chopped**

 Place haddock in baking dish and season with pepper. Combine lemon juice and oil; brush on fish. Separate onion slices into rings and arrange on top of fish; pour remaining lemon-oil mixture over fish. Bake at 400 degrees for 5 minutes. Arrange orange slices over onions, sprinkle parsley over top and bake for 5-8 minutes or until fish is flaky and tender.

The Captain's Sauce For Pasta

Serves: 4-6
Prep Time: 40-45 minutes

1$^1/_2$	lbs. haddock fillets, cubed
1	10$^3/_4$-oz. can cream of mushroom soup, undiluted
$^1/_2$	cup water
2	2-oz. jars pimento, drained and sliced
$^1/_2$	tsp. salt
$^1/_4$	tsp. pepper
$^1/_8$	tsp. dried dillweed (whole)
1	8-oz. pkg. fettuccine noodles parsley sprigs cherry tomatoes

Combine soup, water, pimento, salt, pepper and dillweed in large skillet; stir until well-blended. Cover and bring to a boil. Reduce heat and add haddock. Cover and simmer for 10 minutes, stirring occasionally. Uncover and simmer for an additional 5 minutes or until fish flakes easily when tested with fork. Cook fettuccine according to package directions; drain and transfer to serving platter. Pour haddock sauce over fettuccine and toss lightly to mix. Garnish with parsley sprigs and cherry tomatoes. Serve immediately.

Meals Of The South

Southern Comforts

South Carolina's governor said to North Carolina's governor, "It's a long time between drinks" in the South. But it's rarely a long time between meals. And, as Jimmy Carter noted, " ... differences don't make us weak. They're the source of our strength ... " This applies to "Southern food." You don't get little puddles of nouveau adult baby food in the South. You get solid fried food and wonderfully sweet desserts perfectly designed to compliment fresh fish dishes.

Sensibly enough, catch-and-release isn't big in the South save for bass boaters, offshore fishermen and those wise enough not to bite into a tarpon or bonefish, step on a gaff topsail catfish or sit on a fire-ant hill. "Catchin' a mess" of fish to eat seems the usual, and the best reason to spend time on the reservoir, river or lake. However, it's vital to

Largemouths like this one that has just taken this angler's bait have fueled the reputation of the waters created by the Santee Dam as major bassin' holes.

realize the South no longer lives by grits alone.
Today's South seems to be an international environment gastronomically, as well as in other ways. You enjoy sophisticated French dishes in Atlanta and the Louisiana version, Creole Cooking in New Orleans. Add Cajun food in rural Louisiana, the Caribbean flavors of Cuba and other islands in the stream and, even without the Mexican traditions of Texas, there are enough different kinds of food to put on the odd pound or 10!

Southern diversity started when the French in Louisiana largely were tossed out of Canada by the British. It extended to the Spanish in Florida left over from fountain hunting days, and the newer Cubans. Then there's the herd of Tennessee folk who closed up shop, left their lien holders and put up a sign, "Gone to Texas." Add the old New

Englander mooring out his schooner in a Florida cove to rest on the "run to home" end of the triangular trade of Revolutionary War times, and the South does not seem as much a melting pot as a fine gumbo spiced by cultural and "piscatorial" tradition.

Southern Fresh

Such is also the case with fishing. No other part of the country offers such a spicy mix. Cane poles, bobbers and bait take brim from canals and bayous. Bass boaters, the hot-rodders of the fishing world, zoom across huge impoundments in search of largemouths. Overall-clad folks submerge and stick their hands into hollow stumps and, hopefully, the mouths of huge catfish grab on rather than irate water moccasins. Add the fishery that started when the government dammed the river above Charleston to supply more electricity for the Navy yard so that trapped striped bass are common.

Southern Salt

Then consider early big game fishers like Ernest Hemingway whose trips from his home in Key West to the Dry Tortugas could be traced by floating empties. Tarpon fishing, like most other light tackle saltwater methods, started in the South. This was when New England traders, resting in remote bays that are now condo-clad, sought amusement. Southern blades with the same fine madness that sent Pickett's men up the ridge at Gettysburg ventured out in small boats to spear manta rays, which are definitely "fighting" fish! And don't forget bonefish and permit, the delicate ghosts of the flats, that have put smiles on many fishermen's faces. Now that the threat of "blackened fish" is fended off with new regulations, lively redfish and sea trout are also abundant. Channel bass on the Atlantic Coast, and a host of fine species like king mackerel and tuna offer even more variety.

After all, Hemingway fished from his Key West home. So

Flooded timber in the South's reservoirs provide the kind of structure where fish—particularly bass—love to hang out. The trick is to carefully work the structure in and out.

did famous writers like Phillip Wylie whose *Crunch & Des* stories may have done more to popularize gulf fishing than anything else. If Wylie's tales are to be believed, and they seem too funny to doubt, he was also the most unlucky angler since Jonah. His luck was so bad that the Philip Wylie Hard Luck Trophy became a feature at the Greater Miami Fishing Tournament. The trophy was first awarded in 1941. Jim Scully, who wanted an International Game Fish Association record more than life itself, caught a world-record amberjack, only to see the record broken in less than 60 minutes by a friend.

Lusting For Largemouth

However, the largemouth bass has been the king of the South since before Ray Scott started B.A.S.S. and Forrest Wood left guiding to found Ranger Boats. Today, while metallic-fleck-finish bass boats fast enough to run dope boom around huge impoundments built to the twin gods of rural electrification and flood control, let us not forget it was not always so.

Like bungie jumping, tournament fishing should be tried once. For some, it's addictive. That it's as Southern as stock car and swamp buggy racing should be no surprise.

There's a special excitement to the big bucks, big boats and big bass feel of 200 high-speed craft rooster-tailing over a lake to catch fish that are culled down to the best limit, weighed and released. Europeans, it must be noted, have trouble with the logic of this.

Still, there's life after bass boats. While the big impoundments and major shallow lakes like Florida's Okeechobee collect the tournament types and those who prefer going with guides, it's important to realize that much of the best largemouth bass fishing in the South is in lesser-known waters, including farm ponds, bayous, oxbow lakes off rivers and, indeed, brackish coastal waters easily accessible to the angler with a trailered boat. The few deeper lakes, like Lanier which provides Atlanta's drinking water, add a mix of other species; however, the basic bass water of the South is a murky, snag-filled and shallow home for gator and gar. It's certain that such habitat affected the development of the rather indelicate tackle popular in the South.

Brim, Crappies & Shellcrackers
Homer Circle, one of a dozen outdoor writers who lives in Ocala, Florida, says, "I'd rather fish for brim than bass." It's been suggested that if brim ("bluegills" to Yankees) got as big as bass you'd need saltwater-weight gear to take one. It's common knowledge, at least in the South, that these fish taste better than any other freshwater options. In most parts of the South, they're easy to catch during spring and fall and are readily available all year. Southerners marvel at "bass mania" because such a delicious alternative exists everywhere. Southerners also fry their fish outside in big kettles. This keeps the oil temperatures up so that fish will cook fast.

Much of the best panfishing in the South is on mini waters that offer pleasures of their own. Leave the pup home, though. In the deep South, duck hunters don't use retrievers because "gators can get'um."

Catfish Considered
Southern catfish, like Southern food, are hearty, filling and not particularly attractive. Fried chicken, fried fish, grits and the staple biscuits and gravy all seem rather monochrome. Catfish don't jump, don't usually hit lures, don't require exotic tackle and don't mess with fishermen's minds. They're just there.

Southern catfish anglers seem equally matter-of-fact. Set and trot lines, cane poles, john boats and baits that may announce their presence at 50 yards seem standard.

However, catfish are so delicious that their raising has become a cottage industry in the South second only to small-town speed traps in the days before freeways.

Time For Tarpon

Southern bloods who harpooned manta rays from small skiffs in the years before what Southerners call "The War Between the States" left legacies of bravery. In 1875, the chief outdoor magazine of the day, *Forest And Stream*, tempted readers with tales of tarpon: " ... it is rarely taken on hook and line, as it generally carries away the tackle, however strong." In 1878, Dr. Henshall, a famous authority on black bass, claimed tarpon catches on a heavy green-heart (a popular wooden salmon fly rod) with " ... large, gaudy flies." Until 1900, however, the most common means of tarpon fishing would have suited Moby Dick fans who would have loved to perch in the bow of a skiff poled along the brackish shallows until they came within spear range of resting fish!

By the late 1880's it's estimated that less than 100 tarpon were landed a year, and it's certain that their bright scales fetched 10 to 25 cents apiece. There were a host of conflicting claims about the first tarpon taken with a rod and reel. Tarpon seem rather mysterious; current records are quite hazy, too.

By the 1900s, an astonishing operation existed near Boca Grande, which is still a tarpon hotspot. A huge houseboat called Hughes' Floating Hotel offered anglers both day and night tarpon fishing. Most of these early fishermen used sewn mullets and other baits, and copious chumming seemed the rule.

Tackle evolved, too. Vom Hofe reels, so central to East Coast striper action, burned up anglers' thumbs—you had a leather thumb stall instead of an internal drag! (Without a free spool, rapidly turning handles could lacerate fingers.)

Tarpon clearly tested the primitive tackle and techniques of the time. "High-tech" in those days meant agate guides' Ashaway lines.

The many bubbles and land booms and busts that sent snowbirds South brought in fishing methods and gear from the East and Midwest. Emigrants quickly discovered that their favorite freshwater tackle and techniques would, with a careful selection of the proper spot and some attention to the likely size of tarpon sought, do the job. Best of all, Southern fishermen learned that the tarpon action peaked outside the usual winter tourist season, so locals enjoyed the best of the action.

Wartime Stripers

Think of stripers and you might consider Cape Cod beach buggies parked behind a line of surfcasters during a bass blitz when seagulls dipped and shrieked over baitfish chased into the shallows. Even though stripers did run all the way to Florida (and there's even a program to reintroduce stripers into Texas coastal waters), you think more of channel than striped bass, or "rocks" in Southern climates.

This changed because of World War II. In the rush to complete dams impounding Lakes Moultrie and Marion in South Carolina, the spring spawning run of stripers found itself largely trapped.

Suddenly stripers looked like the final solution to overpopulation of bait like threadfin shad. With 80 to 100 miles of free-flowing stream to float their eggs into impoundments, stripers didn't need saltwater. Stripers were then easily stocked, mostly in the West, and controlled. It was also discovered that inflows from cool streams could do the same job. Striper mania!

Freshwater fishermen who were happy with the odd 10-pound largemouth were suddenly hooking 20-pound stripers on topwater lures—and in bunches! States rushed to build hatcheries. Tennessee, for example, stuck 1 million stripers a year into each of six impoundments. Clubs and contests abounded. Then, as the initial dominant age class of stripers thinned, baitfish schools and species like trout that spent time in the middle of lakes, began to decrease in size. In most waters where they are present, stripers still are the largest gamefish.

Remembering Redfish

Even though tarpon may offer the best photo opportunities and gaff-topsail catfish seem to be the ubiquitous Southern fish, redfish and pompano remain gastronomic champs on the coast. Even Paul Prudhome couldn't find enough redfish to blacken skillets and kitchen ceilings nationwide; therefore, some savvy Southerners started to sell drum as redfish. Fortunately, regulations changed fast enough to ensure good supplies of redfish indefinitely.

Pompano, the Gulf Coast's answer to the best yellow perch ever caught in the Midwest, got less pressure as their delicate flesh simply doesn't ship well. If you're ever on the gulf and can manage a batch of pompano with sand flies and other small baits, melt some butter and gently poach some pompano with a squeeze of lemon. You'll enjoy America's most underrated fish delicacy.

Georgia On My Mind

Serves: 4-6

Atlanta combines the sophistication of a big city with the traditions of the South. This menu offers a sophisticated hors d'oeuvre best served on toothpicks, a coastal taste of bass and the country taste of rutabaga, a most underrated vegetable. As is often the case in the South, dinner ends with a sweet cake guaranteed lethal to diets!

Appetizer: Golden-Fried Artichoke Hearts

6-8   **fresh or frozen artichoke hearts**
$1/4$ **cup olive oil**
$1/2$ **cup flour**
$1/8$ **tsp. salt**
$1/8$ **tsp. pepper**
$1/4$ **tsp. thyme**
1   **large egg, beaten**
$1/4$ **cup butter**

Remove lower leaves and chokes from artichokes. Cut artichokes into halves. Add olive oil to 10-inch skillet over medium heat. Combine flour, salt, pepper and thyme. Dip each artichoke in flour mixture, then in beaten egg. Fry artichokes until golden brown on both sides. Drain remaining oil; add butter. Saute artichokes in butter until done.

Salad: Romaine Salad With Strawberries

1   **head romaine lettuce**
4   **red cabbage leaves, shredded**
$1/2$ **small red or mild Valdosta onions, sliced**
1   **cup fresh sliced strawberries**

Poppy-Seed Dressing:
$1/4$ **cup honey**
1   **tsp. dry mustard**
$1/2$ **tsp. paprika**
5   **T. lemon or lime juice**
    grated peel from half lemon or lime
$3/4$ **cup oil**

2　T. poppy seeds
　　salt and pepper to taste

In blender, prepare poppy-seed dressing: Combine honey, mustard, paprika, lemon juice and peel. Blend well. Slowly add oil in a thin stream, until well blended. Stir in poppy seeds and salt and pepper. Refrigerate for 30 minutes. (Makes about 1 cup and will keep up to 5 days.) In salad bowl, tear lettuce into bite-sized pieces. Arrange cabbage, onions and strawberries. Pour on poppy-seed dressing, toss and serve. (Note: Strawberries add a nice sweet and tart taste to salad.)

Entree: Bass Fillets Piquant

2　lbs. bass fillets or steaks (channel,
　　black, or striped), cut 1 inch thick
2　T. minced onions
1/8　tsp. pepper
1/2　tsp. salt
3　T. lemon juice
1/4　cup melted butter
1/4　tsp. ground or 1/2 tsp. fresh minced savory
1/4　tsp. dried or 1/2 tsp. fresh marjoram
2　T. fresh minced parsley

In bowl, combine onions, pepper, salt, lemon juice, butter, savory, marjoram and parsley. Heat broiler. Pour half of onion mixture in baking pan. Lay bass on top. Broil 6 inches from broiler for 15-18 minutes or until fish flakes when tested with fork. Baste once with sauce from pan. Arrange fish on platter and top with remaining sauce.

Side Dish: Mashed Rutabagas

2　lbs. rutabagas
1/2　tsp. salt
1　tsp. sugar
2　T. butter
1　tsp. onion powder
1　tsp. paprika
　　dillweed

Peel and cut rutabagas into ¹/₂-inch cubes. In saucepan, add enough water to cover rutabagas. Add salt and sugar; bring to a boil over high heat and cook for 20-25 minutes or until tender. Drain rutabagas. In bowl, mash rutabagas. Stir in butter, onion powder and paprika. Sprinkle dillweed over top and serve.

Dessert: Chocolate Upside Down Cake

1	**cup flour**
³/₄	**cup sugar**
2	**tsp. baking powder**
¹/₄	**tsp. salt**
5	**tsp. cocoa**
¹/₂	**cup milk**
1	**tsp. vanilla**
2	**T. melted butter**
1	**cup chopped pecans**
1	**cup boiling water**

Topping:

¹/₂	**cup sugar**
¹/₂	**cup brown sugar**
¹/₄	**cup cocoa**

In bowl, mix flour, sugar, baking powder, salt and cocoa. Stir in milk and vanilla. Add melted butter and pecans. Pour into greased baking pan. Combine sugar, brown sugar and cocoa. Spread sugar mixture over cake batter. Pour 1 cup boiling water over top of cake. Bake at 350 degrees for 30-35 minutes or until cake is done when tested with toothpick. Serve warm or cold with ice cream or whip cream.

Caribbean Comforts
Serves: 4-6

Florida's Caribbean-style dishes suit tropical nights. This dish, a summer favorite, works well with any cooked, flaky fish. It's even better with conch or a mix of fish and shrimp. However, do not make fritters in an electric skillet at a buffet-style party. Someone will always burn fingers in their haste to take more than their fair share! A big green salad suits this menu.

Appetizer: Shrimp Kabobs

- 1 lb. raw, medium-sized shrimp, peeled
- 3 T. vegetable or olive oil
- 3 T. lemon or lime juice
- 1 T. soy sauce (light)
- 1 garlic clove, mashed
  bamboo or metal skewers
  paprika ("pepper heads" can use hot
  Hungarian paprika)

Mix oil, lemon juice, soy sauce and mashed garlic in small bowl. Add shrimp and marinate for 2-3 hours. Skewer shrimp and season lightly with paprika. Broil quickly on each side until shrimp turn pink and opaque. Good hot or cold.

Entree: Fab Fish Fritters

- 2 cups cooked flaky firm fish (bass or stripers)
- 2 T. butter
- 4 T. onion, finely chopped
- 2 T. fresh chopped parsley
- 4 T. flour or bread crumbs
- 1/2 cup half-and-half or heavy cream
- 1/4 tsp. salt
- 1 1/2 tsp. lemon-pepper seasoning
- 1 egg, slightly beaten
  vegetable oil
- 3 T. flour
- 1 egg
- 2 tsp. water
- 1/2 cup dry bread crumbs

In skillet, melt butter over medium heat and saute onion and parsley for 2 minutes. Stir in 4 T. flour or bread crumbs. Blend in half-and-half, salt and lemon-pepper. Cook over low heat until mixture thickens, stirring constantly. Remove from heat. Stir in fish and 1 beaten egg. Mix and refrigerate for 30 minutes, or until chilled. Heat 3-inch-deep oil to 375 degrees in deep fryer or saucepan. On waxed paper, spread remaining 3 T. flour evenly. Beat remaining egg with water in separate bowl. Place bread crumbs in separate bowl. Drop 1 T. of fish mixture onto flour. Roll fish to coat and shape into balls, then dip in egg mixture and roll in bread crumbs. Fry 5-6 balls at a time, turning occasionally until golden brown (about 3 minutes). Drain on paper towels. Keep warm in 175-degree oven. Serve with your favorite tartar sauce. (Makes about 36 fritters).

Side Dish: Fried Bananas

6	**medium bananas**
1/2	**cup orange juice**
1	**T. lemon or lime juice**
4	**T. butter or oil**

Peel bananas and cut lengthwise into 1/2-inch slices. Combine orange and lemon juice. Heat skillet over medium heat and melt butter. Dip bananas in juice with slotted spoon. Fry bananas until golden brown (about 4 minutes), drain on paper towel and serve on warm platter. (To serve as a dessert: Combine 2 T. brown sugar and 1 T. Grand Marnier with orange/lemon juice and place bananas in buttered casserole. Pour juice mixture over bananas and dot with butter. Bake about 10 minutes at 400 degrees. Sprinkle grated coconut over top and serve.)

Dessert: Pier House Key-Lime Pie

4	**eggs, separated**
1	**14-oz. can sweetened condensed milk**
1/2	**cup Key Lime Juice (fresh or bottled)**
1/2	**tsp. cream of tartar**
1	**graham cracker crust**

Meringue:

4	**egg whites**
4	**T. sugar**

Heat oven to 325 degrees. Beat egg yolks at high speed until thick and light in color. Stop mixer. Add condensed milk. Mix at slow speed. Add half of lime juice and cream of tartar. Mix. Add remaining lime juice and mix until well blended. Pour into graham-cracker crust and bake for 10-15 minutes, or until set. Center of pie will be firm and dry to touch. Freeze for at least 3 hours before topping with meringue. For meringue, heat egg whites in double boiler with sugar, stirring frequently, until at 110 degrees. Then beat on high speed until peaks are formed. Top frozen pie with meringue and return to freezer until ready to serve. (Note: This is one of the simplest and best tasting Key Lime recipes. Though you can use fresh or bottled lime or lemon juice, Key Lime juice makes enough difference to justify the extra cost. This special recipe is still served at Pier House, One Duval St., Key West, Florida.)

Catfish Considered
Serves: 4

Most catfish, as well as crayfish, sold in the United States come from the South. This wonderful Southern menu works indoors; however, for those with white kitchens, you may want to blacken your fish outside! Cool your crayfish, and prepare the salad and cornbread early. Dessert assembles at the last minute. (Note: To really get into the crayfish, you can use the traditional, if inelegant, "newspaper on the picnic table" method.) Deep-fried catfish should be served on a metal roasting pan because the fish is too big for a plate. The lack of frills like side dishes and table cloths often signals fabulous fish.

Appetizer: Crayfish Dill

50	**fresh crayfish**
3	**T. salt**
4	**qts. water**
2	**T. dry dillweed**
	melted butter
	lemon wedges

Rinse crayfish. Add salt to water and boil dillweed for 5 minutes. Add crayfish and cook for 5-7 minutes, or until crayfish shells turn red. Drain and serve whole to friends with melted butter and lemon wedges. Serve cold, shell and shuck tails and claws for picky visitors.

Salad: Broccoli Salad

1	lb. broccoli flowerettes
2	T. butter
2	T. pine nuts
1/4	lb. fresh sliced mushrooms

Dressing:

5	T. olive oil
3	T. lemon juice
3	T. chopped green onion
1/2	tsp. garlic powder
1/4	tsp. dry mustard
1/8	tsp. salt
1/4	tsp. pepper

Cook broccoli in 1-inch-deep boiling water for 5 minutes; then rinse with cold water and drain. In skillet over medium heat, melt butter and lightly brown pine nuts. In salad bowl, combine broccoli, pine nuts and mushrooms; refrigerate until cold. In jar, mix dressing ingredients. Just before serving, shake dressing and pour over salad; toss lightly.

Entree: Blackened Catfish

6-7 1/2	lbs. catfish fillets
2	tsp. paprika
1/4	tsp. dry basil leaves
1/4	tsp. thyme
6	bay leaves, crushed
1/2	tsp. garlic powder
2	T. salt
1/4	tsp. pepper
1/4	tsp. cayenne pepper
1/4	tsp. white pepper
2	sticks butter

Pat fillets dry and chill for 1 hour in refrigerator. Combine remaining ingredients, except butter, in bowl. Sprinkle seasonings on both sides of each fillet and place fillets on waxed paper. Melt butter in separate pan. Heat cast-iron skillet, fish fryer or Dutch oven until bottom is nearly red hot. Dip fillets in melted butter to coat and immediately drop them into hot skillet or Dutch oven. Cook just 30-40 seconds or until dark brown, then flip and cook other side for 30-40 seconds. (Fillets will sputter and smoke so prepare this recipe outdoors on a camp stove.) Remove fillets from your blackened pan and serve with leftover melted butter.

Side Dish: Gruyere Onion Corn Bread

	butter
1	egg, beaten
1	cup milk
1/4	cup dry onion flakes
2	T. chopped green chilis
1/4	cup oil
1/2	tsp. salt
1	cup cornmeal
1	cup all-purpose flour
1	T. baking powder
1	cup cream-style corn
3/4	cup shredded Gruyere cheese
	paprika

Butter 8-inch square pan. Heat oven to 375 degrees. In small bowl, combine egg, milk, onion flakes, chilis, oil and salt. In electric mixer or with spoon in medium bowl, combine corn-meal, flour and baking powder. Add corn and mix until blended; then pour in egg mixture and mix thoroughly. Stir in 1/2 cup shredded cheese. Pour batter into prepared pan. Spread remaining cheese on top and sprinkle with paprika. Bake for 40 minutes or until toothpick inserted in center comes out clean.

Dessert: Raspberry Champagne

1	pt. raspberry sherbert
1	cup fresh raspberries
1	small bottle champagne

In dessert glasses, divide sherbert into 4 servings. Top with raspberries. Just before serving, pour 3 T. champagne over each serving. Serve bubbling dessert immediately.

Time For Guests, Family Treats
Serves: 6

Stuffing medium-sized fish to bake sends the cook to join the guests—a Southern tradition when many had help at home. This recipe works well with all bass, decent-sized saltwater and freshwater trout, offshore bottom-fish and more. It's an adaption of a dish popular on the Texas and Mexican coasts. It got its name when we asked Mabel, my uncle's cook, what she called the dish. "Basic Baked" seems a fine description. The pecan basil salad, and, in particular, the matching dressing can also stand alone as a light luncheon snack. Strawberry Pecan Torte comes to us from a Creole restaurant in New Orleans. You don't need vegetables or an appetizer with this filling meal.

Salad: Walnut Basil Salad

- 1 **head lettuce**
- 2 **medium tomatoes, sliced**
- 1 **avocado, sliced**
- 1 **cup fresh mushrooms, sliced**
  croutons (see recipe below)

Pecan Basil Dressing:
- 2 **tsp. mustard**
- 3 **T. rice vinegar**
- 3 **T. dry basil**
- 1/2 **tsp. sugar**
- 1/2 **cup salad oil or olive oil**
- 1/4 **cup pecans, finely chopped or coarsely ground**
  salt and pepper to taste

Tear lettuce leaves into serving-sized pieces and spread on individual salad dishes. Arrange sliced tomatoes, avocado and mushrooms on top. Combine mustard, vinegar, basil and sugar in food processor and blend for 30 seconds. Then continue to blend as you add oil in a steady stream. Remove dressing from blender and stir in nuts. Season with salt and pepper. Use cold ingredients if it is served immediately, or refrigerate.

Homemade Garlic Croutons

 2 T. oil
 2 T. butter
 4 bread slice (day-old or air-dried bread),
   cut into 1/4 to 1/2-inch cubes.
 1 tsp. garlic powder
   your favorite herbs and spices (dill,
   tarragon, basil, onion)
   Parmesan cheese (optional)

Melt oil and butter over medium heat. Add remaining ingredients and cook until bread browns.

Entree: Basic Baked

 3-4 lbs. whole fish
 1/4 lb. butter
 1 medium onion, chopped
 3 celery stalks, chopped
 1 tsp. ground sage
 1 tsp. thyme leaves
 1 tsp. dry parsley
 2 cups cooked rice
 1 6-oz. can green olives with pimentos
  salt and pepper

Clean fish, remove fins and scale. (You can leave tail on, spread it and keep it from browning with a foil shield. The head can also be left on and the eye replaced with an olive.) Pat fish dry and place on greased baking dish. Heat oven to 350 degrees. Melt butter in skillet over medium heat. Saute chopped onion and celery until tender. Add seasonings, rice and drained olives. Mix thoroughly, then stuff fish. Add extra rice to buttered casserole and bake with fish; baste with liquid. Season fish with salt and pepper and cook for 1 hour or until fish flakes when tested with fork. (You can refrigerate and cool stuffing if made in advance.)

Dessert: Strawberry Pecan Torte

 4 eggs
 1/2 cup sugar

1   cup sifted flour
1   tsp. vanilla
¹/₂   cup pecans, finely chopped

Filling/Topping:
1   pt. strawberries, sliced (keep a few whole)
1   cup heavy cream
2   T. powdered sugar
1   tsp. vanilla

Heat oven to 350 degrees. Grease 8-inch spring-form pan and dust with granulated sugar, then flour. Whip eggs, ¹/₂ cup sugar and vanilla until thick enough to leave ribbon trail when beater is lifted. Gradually fold 1 cup flour and pecans into egg mixture. Pour mixture into prepared pan and cook for 30 minutes or until cake springs back when lightly pressed with finger. Place cake onto wire rack to cool. Whip cream, powdered sugar and vanilla. Split cake layers in half (sawing with a thread is easier than cutting with a knife). Fill middle of cake with two-thirds of whipped cream and half of sliced strawberries. Top with remaining cream and strawberries. Garnish with a few whole strawberries and serve.

Creole Confections
Serves 6-8

The Creoles, like the French, do not see crepes as special; however, they use them as wrappers to stretch leftover stews or cooked fruits. Crepes impress. They are as easy to make as pancakes once you understand the texture of the liquid and the need to let the batter set. You can also make, cool and separate crepes with squares of waxed paper for freezing. Fish seem particularly well-suited for the delicate taste and texture of crepes. If you have crepe leftovers from the following entree recipe, you can use them for the Apple Normandy dessert.

Salad: Spinach Caesar Salad

³/₄   cup olive oil
1   garlic clove, crushed
1   bunch spinach

$^1/_4$ **teaspoon salt**
       freshly ground black pepper to taste
  2   **cups day-old bread, cut into $^1/_2$-inch cubes**
  1   **egg**
$^1/_4$ **cup lemon juice**
$^1/_2$ **cup Parmesan cheese**

Add oil to garlic and let stand for 2 hours. Remove stems from spinach and tear into bite-sized pieces. Place spinach pieces in salad bowl. Add salt and pepper. Heat $^1/_4$ cup garlic oil in skillet. Add bread cubes and saute until brown on all sides. Drain croutons on paper towel. Add remaining garlic oil to spinach and toss until leaves are well coated. Break egg into center of spinach, add lemon juice and toss until well-mixed and creamy. Add Parmesan cheese and croutons. Toss lightly.

Entree: Fish And Shrimp Crepes

Basic Crepe Batter (makes 16 crepes):
   1   **egg**
   1   **egg yolk**
   1   **cup flour**
       pinch salt
$1^1/_4$ **cups milk**
   1   **T. butter or oil**

Cheese Sauce:
$^1/_4$ **cup flour**
  1   **stick butter, softened**
  2   **cups milk**
$^1/_2$ **cup half-and-half or heavy cream**
  1   **tsp. onion powder**
$^1/_4$ **tsp. salt**
$^1/_4$ **tsp. white pepper**
$^1/_4$ **cup grated Swiss cheese**

Filling:
  2   **cups cooked flaked fish**
  2   **cups cooked shrimp**
  1   **cup celery, thinly sliced**
  2   **T. butter**
  2   **T. bread crumbs**

To make crepes, beat egg and egg yolk together in small dish. Sift flour and salt into bowl. Add eggs and slowly pour in half of milk (to prevent lumps), stirring constantly. Slowly add melted butter or oil. Beat well until smooth. Add remaining milk and stir until smooth. Cover and let stand at room temperature for at least 30 minutes before using. Batter should be the consistency of light cream (if too thick, add milk). Over medium heat, place 6-inch pan and brush it lightly with oil. Pour 3-4 T. batter into pan and immediately roll batter around to evenly coat bottom of pan. Pour out excess batter. Cook only until bottom of crepe is golden brown (about 25 seconds). Turn crepe over and cook for about 10 seconds more or until brown. Stack crepes on warm plate or cover in warm oven until needed.

To make cheese sauce, mix flour with butter until smooth; then roll into ball. Heat milk in saucepan over medium heat. Add butter ball and stir until mixture thickens. Add half-and-half, onion powder, salt and pepper; simmer for 3-5 minutes or until sauce warms. Add cheese. Cook until cheese melts and sauce is medium-thick.

To prepare filling, combine fish, 1 cup shrimp and celery with 1/4 cup cheese sauce in bowl. Fill each crepe with 2-3 T. of filling. Tuck edges of crepe under to form smooth roll and place side by side until dish is full. Cover crepes with remaining cheese sauce. Melt 2 T. butter and mix in bread crumbs. Sprinkle bread crumbs over top of crepes. Garnish with reserved shrimp before baking 30 minutes at 350 degrees.

Dessert: Apple Normandy

2	T. butter
2	large apples, peeled and diced into 1/4-inch thick cubes
1/4	tsp. cinnamon
2	T. dark brown sugar
8-10	warm crepes (see crepe recipe)
1/4	cup light or dark corn syrup
1/4	cup apple liqueur or brandy

Melt butter in large frying pan or chafing dish until brown. Add apples and cook until tender and brown over medium heat.

Sprinkle cinnamon and brown sugar over apples and continue to cook for 3 minutes. In same skillet, spoon 1 T. apple mixture in center of each warm crepe. Roll crepes like cigars and push to sides of pan. When ready to serve, add syrup and brandy to crepes. Using caution, ignite with match to "flambe." Baste crepes with sauce and serve immediately.

It's Fish And Chips, Y'all
Serves: 4-6

Since the British were the first settlers in the South, it's not surprising that traditional British Fish and Chips have become transmuted in Southern hands. Most experts agree you should only cook a few pieces of fish and, in separate oil, a few potatoes at the same time. Large amounts of fish or chips cool the oil and get greasy. A coleslaw complements these large succulent chips that taste much better than most French fries. These dishes are simple, quick, easy and delicious! So serve them with a rather fancy-looking strawberry dessert that's easy to prepare before the meal.

Salad: Poppy-Seed Coleslaw

- **4 cups red cabbage, finely shredded**
- **4 cups green cabbage, finely shredded**
- **4 green onions, sliced**
- **1 small red bell pepper, cut into 1/4-inch thin strips**
- **1 small green pepper, cut into 1/4-inch thin strips**

Dressing:
- **1/3 cup mayonnaise**
- **2/3 cup sour cream**
- **1 T. red or white wine vinegar**
- **1 tsp. Dijon mustard**
- **1/4 tsp. salt**
- **1/2 tsp. pepper**
- **1/2 tsp. sugar**
- **1 T. poppy seed**

Combine dressing ingredients and blend well. Refrigerate until ready to use. In large bowl, add red and green cabbage, onions and red and green peppers. Pour dressing over cabbage salad and toss well to coat.

Entree: Southern Fish Fry A.K.A. Fish & Chips

**2   lbs. fish fillets, steaks or chunks
    oil or shortening**

Batter:
1   cup flour
1   egg
1   cup milk or beer
1/2   tsp. salt
1/4   tsp. white pepper
2   T. dry onion flakes

Chips:
**   potatoes**
4-6   cups oil or shortening

Combine batter ingredients. In deep fryer or heavy saucepan, add oil 3 inches deep. Wash and dry fish with paper towels so they will pick up batter. Heat oil or shortening to 375 degrees. Drop piece of bread in oil to test (bread should turn golden in less than 1 minute). Coat fillets completely with batter. Carefully submerge fish into oil and cook for 4-7 minutes, depending upon thickness of fish. Drain fish on paper towels and serve hot.

To make chips, slice potatoes into 1/2-inch-thick lengthwise wedges. Heat oil or shortening to 375 degrees in separate deep-fat fryer or heavy saucepan. Add potatoes and cook until golden brown (about 4 minutes). Serve fish and chips with malt vinegar or lemon-tarragon sauce (see following recipe).

Lemon-Tarragon Sauce:

2	**T. butter**		**1**	**T. grated lemon peel**
1	**T. flour**		**1**	**tsp. lemon juice**
3/4	**cup clam juice**		**1/2**	**tsp. sugar**
1	**T. tarragon leaves**			

Melt butter in small saucepan and stir in flour and clam juice. Add lemon peel, lemon juice, sugar and tarragon. Stir and cook for about 5 minutes over medium heat until sauce thickens slightly. Serve with fish immediately.

Dessert: Grand Marnier Strawberry Mousse

1	lb. fresh strawberries
1	T. Grand Marnier liqueur or orange juice
1/4	cup sugar
2	egg whites
1 1/4	cup heavy cream
2	T. powdered sugar

Wash and hull strawberries. (Reserve 6 large strawberries for topping.) Crush strawberries and mix with liqueur and sugar. Beat egg whites until stiff. In separate bowl, beat cream until thick. Add powdered sugar and continue to beat until stiff. Fold 1 cup cream into mashed strawberries. (Reserve remaining 1/4 cup of whipped cream for topping.) Fold egg whites into strawberry mixture. Spoon dessert into serving dishes or wine glasses. Refrigerate for 2 or more hours. Top with reserved cream and strawberries.

Recipes For:

Halibut

Jack

Lingcod

Mackerel

Mahi-Mahi

A-Wards' Alaskan Halibut Supreme

Serves: 6
Prep Time: 1 hour

2-3 lbs. halibut roast
1 whole Dungeness crab
1 cup sour cream or plain yogurt
1 cup mayonnaise or plain yogurt
1 T. lemon juice
1 T. lemon-pepper seasoning
mushrooms, chopped
dillseed to taste
parsley flakes to taste
1-1¹/₂ cups cheddar cheese,
grated (optional)

Butcher and break whole crab from shell and remove viscera.
Cook legs and body meat for 10-15 minutes in boiling water.
Remove crabmeat from heat and cool. Shred crabmeat and
combine with sour cream and mayonnaise to form paste-like
mixture. Add remaining ingredients, except cheese. Place halibut roast in baking dish and cut deep slices ³/₄ inches apart
throughout roast. Stuff crabmeat mixture into slices and dab
remaining mixture on top of roast. Grate cheddar cheese over
roast. Cover and bake at 375 degrees for 15-20 minutes.

Robert Ward
Anchor Point, Alaska

Mexicali Grilled Halibut

Serves: 4
Prep Time: 1 hour, 30 minutes

1	**lb. halibut steaks or fillets**
¹/₃	**cup lime juice**
3	**garlic cloves, minced**
1	**T. oil**
¹/₄	**cup beer**
1	**T. parsley, chopped**
2	**tsp. spicy mustard**
¹/₄	**tsp. pepper**
2	**tomatoes, peeled, seeded and chopped**
¹/₄	**cup green onion, chopped**
3	**T. green chilis, diced**
¹/₂	**cup green pepper, diced**

Combine lime juice, garlic, oil, beer, parsley, mustard and pepper to form marinade. Place halibut steaks in dish and pour marinade over top. Cover and marinate in refrigerator for 1 hour, turning once. In separate bowl, combine tomatoes, onion, chilis and green pepper to make sauce. Let stand for 20 minutes before using. Drain halibut and reserve marinade. Place halibut on lightly oiled grill 4-5 inches from hot coals. Cook for 4-5 minutes, baste with marinade and turn. Cook for an additional 4-5 minutes or until halibut is flaky and tender. Top with tomato sauce.

Yankee Halibut

Serves: 8
Prep Time: 1 hour

1	2-lb. whole halibut, dressed	2	cups celery, sliced
12	carrots, peeled and cut lengthwise	1/3	cup water
		2	bay leaves
8	potatoes, peeled and quartered	1	garlic clove, minced
		2	T. butter, melted
10	small white onions	1/4	tsp. pepper

Place halibut in large, lightly oiled baking dish and surround with prepared carrots, potatoes, onions and celery. Combine water, bay leaves and garlic; pour mixture over fish and vegetables. Brush fish and vegetables with melted butter and sprinkle pepper over top. Cover with foil and bake at 400 degrees for 45 minutes or until fish is flaky and vegetables are tender.

Micro-Easy Halibut Steaks

Serves: 4
Prep Time: 20-25 minutes

4	halibut steaks		Alouette cheese or
1/4	cup mayonnaise		other soft creamed
1/2	tsp. garlic powder		cheese with herbs
1	4-oz. container	2	T. sweet pickle relish
2	T. fresh chives, minced		

Arrange halibut steaks in 7x12-inch buttered baking dish. In small bowl, combine all ingredients (except chives); blend well. Spread mixture over each steak. Cover with vented plastic wrap and microwave on high for 7-8 minutes or until centers of steaks begin flaking when pierced with fork. Turn dish once during baking. Sprinkle chives over top and microwave (uncovered) on high for $2^{1/2}$ more minutes. Cover and let stand for 5 minutes before serving.

Poached Alaskan Halibut With Cucumber Sauce

Serves: 4-6
Prep Time: 30 minutes, 1 hour

1¹/₂   lbs. halibut steaks (thawed)
**   3   cups water**
¹/₂   cup white wine
**   1   bay leaf**
**   dash thyme, crushed**

Creamy Cucumber Dill Sauce:
**   1   cup sour cram**
³/₄   cup cucumber, finely chopped
**   1   T. vinegar**
¹/₄   tsp. dillweed

Combine water, wine, bay leaf and thyme; bring to a boil. Add halibut and reduce heat. Cover and simmer for 10 minutes per inch of thickness or until fish flakes when tested with fork. Gently remove halibut and drain. Serve hot or chilled with creamy dill sauce. To make dill sauce, combine sour cream, cucumber, vinegar and dillweed. Cover and refrigerate for at least 1 hour before serving.

Patricia Severe
Kenai, Alaska

Smoked Fish Pate Appetizers

Serves: several (yields 2 cups)
Prep Time:

1/3 lb. smoked jack fish
1 pt. cherry tomatoes
1 8-oz. pkg. cream cheese, softened
2 T. fresh parsley, minced
1 T. fresh dill, minced
2 green onions, minced
2 T. lemon juice
salt and pepper to taste
dash paprika (optional)
dash chives or parsley, minced (optional)

Rinse cherry tomatoes under running water and carefully slice off tops. Scoop pulp out with small serrated knife or spoon. In food processor, chop fish. Add remaining ingredients (except paprika and chives) and blend mixture until smooth. Add 1-2 T. milk to thin mixture if needed. Fill each tomato shell with fish mixture and refrigerate. Before serving, garnish with paprika or finely minced chives or parsley.

Jack Fillets Marinara

Serves: 4
Prep Time: 1 hour, 15 minutes

1	lb. jack fillets
1/3	cup onions, chopped
1	garlic clove, minced
2	T. oil
1	16-oz. can tomatoes, undrained
1	bay leaf
1	tsp. dried oregano
1/2	tsp. dried parsley flakes
1/2	tsp. dried basil
1/4	tsp. salt
1/2	tsp. lemon-pepper seasoning
1/2	cup Parmesan cheese, grated
1/2	cup mozzarella cheese, grated

Saute onion and garlic in oil until tender. Add tomatoes and seasonings; simmer for 15 minutes. Place fish fillets in buttered baking dish and pour sauce over fish. Bake at 375 degrees for 25 minutes or until fish flakes easily when tested with fork, basting often with sauce. Sprinkle cheese over fish and place under broiler for 3-5 minutes or until cheese is bubbly. Serve with crusty French bread and tossed salad.

Micro-Easy Chinese Lingcod

Serves: 4
Prep Time: 15-25 minutes

1	lb. lingcod fillets
1	T. butter
2	tsp. lemon juice
1/2	tsp. ginger
1	T. brown sugar
3	tsp. cornstarch
2	T. water
3	T. sherry
2	T. soy sauce
1	cup celery, sliced
1/2	cup white mushrooms
1/2	cup pineapple chunks

Place lingcod in non-metallic baking dish. Dot with butter and sprinkle lemon juice and ginger over top. Cover and microwave on high for 3-4 minutes or until fish is flaky and tender. Rotate dish at midpoint of cooking time. In large container, combine brown sugar and cornstarch. Add water, sherry and soy sauce; microwave on high for 1 minute or until thickened, stirring at midpoint of cooking time. Stir in celery, mushrooms and pineapple; microwave for 2 minutes. Pour mixture over lingcod and serve.

Flavorful Stuffed Lingcod

Serves: 6
Prep Time: 35-45 minutes

2	**1¹/₂-lb. lingcod steaks**
¹/₄	**cup onions, chopped**
¹/₂	**cup fresh mushrooms, sliced**
2	**T. butter**
¹/₄	**tsp. dried thyme**
¹/₄	**cup fresh parsley, minced**
¹/₂	**fresh parsley, minced**
¹/₂	**cup fresh bread crumbs**
¹/₄	**cup half-and-half or light cream**
	salt and pepper to taste
1	**tsp. curry (optional)**
	paprika to taste
	citrus to taste

Saute onions and mushrooms in butter until soft. Add thyme and
parsley; cook for 1 minute. To make stuffing, combine bread
crumbs, half-and-half and salt and pepper with sauteed onions
and mushrooms. Spread stuffing mix over 1 steak in buttered
baking dish. Top with second steak, sandwich-style. Bake at 425
degrees for 20 minutes or until fish flakes easily when tested
with fork. Serve sandwich with basic white sauce in which 1 tsp.
curry per 1 cup sauce has been added. Garnish with paprika
and citrus.

'Just in Thyme' Lingcod

Serves: 8
Prep Time: 1 hour, 20-30 minutes

2 lbs. lingcod fillets or steaks
1/2 tsp. dried mustard
1/2 cup onion, chopped
2 T. oil
1 tsp. thyme
1 tsp. rosemary
1/2 tsp. pepper
1/4 tsp. salt
1/2 cup lemon juice
1 garlic clove, minced

Combine all ingredients to form marinade and marinate fish for 1 hour, turning once. Remove fish from marinade and grill or broil 4 inches from heat for 15 minutes; turn and cook for 5-10 more minutes or until fish is tender and flaky when tested with fork.

Baked Mackerel Provencal

Serves: 4
Prep Time: 45-55 minutes

1¹/₂	lbs. mackerel fillets
2	garlic cloves, crushed
¹/₂	tsp. hot pepper flakes
¹/₂	tsp. chili powder
¹/₂	tsp. dried oregano
¹/₄	tsp. ground cumin
1	16-oz. can stewed tomatoes
1	cup garbanzo beans
1	cup Italian cut green beans (optional)

In medium saucepan, saute garlic lightly. Add remaining ingredients, except beans. Simmer for 5 minutes. Stir in beans.
Preheat oven to 400 degrees. Place fish in large baking dish,
pouring sauce over and around fish. Bake for 20-25 minutes or
until fish flakes easily when tested with fork. Serve with crusty
French bread.

Spicy Steamed Mackerel

Serves: 6
Prep Time: 35-45 minutes

1	3-lb. mackerel, dressed	1	lemon, thinly sliced
1	T. butter, cut into pieces	¹/₄	tsp. pepper
1	tsp. lemon juice	1	tsp. ginger, grated
¹/₂	lb. fresh bamboo shoots	2	T. sherry
1	onion, thinly sliced		

Slice open cavity of mackerel to insert butter, lemon juice, bamboo shoots, onion and lemon slices. Season fish inside and out
with pepper and ginger. Wrap fish loosely in aluminum foil and
place on rack directly over boiling water; add sherry to water.
Cover and steam for 20-30 minutes (don't overcook).

Seafood Lovers Salad

Serves 4-6
Prep Time: 15-20 minutes

6 4-oz.mackerel fillets
4 T. cooking oil
4 T. blackened fish seasoning (combine ground
pepper, paprika and other favorite spices)
5 cups mixed, torn greens
3 T. tarragon vinegar
2 T. dry Italian salad dressing mix

In skillet, heat 1 T. oil; sprinkle fish seasoning on waxed paper. Dredge skinless side of fillets in seasonings. Place fillets, seasoned-side down in hot skillet and cook for 3 minutes or until crisp; turn and cook an additional 1-2 minutes. In sealable jar, combine water, vinegar, remaining oil and dressing mix; shake well to blend. Place greens in bowl and pour on hot dressing; toss to coat. Arrange greens on serving platter and top with cooked mackerel fillets.

Creamy Asparagus Mahi Mahi

Serves: 4
Prep Time: 30-45 minutes

2	**lbs. mahi mahi**
	lemon-pepper
2	**cups cooked rice**
1/2	**lb. asparagus, cooked**
1	**can cream of asparagus soup**
3	**T. sour cream**
1	**T. lemon juice**
	bread crumbs
	lemon slices

Sprinkle lemon-pepper over fish and broil until flaky. In baking dish, place rice, asparagus and fish in alternating layers; set aside. In small bowl, combine soup, sour cream and lemon juice. Add mixture to baking dish. Sprinkle bread crumbs over top and bake at 300 degrees for 20 minutes or until bubbly. Garnish with lemon slices.

Jeff Huelsman
LaVerne, California

Luau Mahi Mahi

Serves: 4
Prep Time: 20-25 minutes

1	**lb. mahi mahi fillets**	**1/8**	**tsp. pepper**
6	**T. flour**	**1**	**T. butter**
1/4	**tsp. onion powder**	**6**	**cashew nuts, chopped**

To make coating mixture, combine flour, onion powder and pepper; dredge mahi mahi. In shallow baking dish, melt butter and add fish, turning to coat. Sprinkle cashew nuts over fish and bake at 400 degrees for 10 minutes or until fish is tender.

Micro-Easy Pacific Island Fish

Serves: 4-6
Prep Time: 20-25 minutes

4-6	4-oz. mahi mahi fillets	1	tsp. prepared mustard
1/2	cup sour cream	1/4	tsp. celery seed
1/2	tsp. fresh horseradish	3/4	cup coleslaw, drained

Rinse fillets and pat dry with paper towels. In small bowl, combine sour cream, horseradish, mustard and celery seed. Spread 1 tsp. of mixture on each fillet. Reserve remaining mixture. Place 2 T. of drained coleslaw on each fillet, spreading evenly. Starting at narrow end, gently roll each fillet (jelly-roll style) and secure ends with toothpicks. Place each fillet in oblong baking dish (preferably with rack) and cover with vented plastic wrap; microwave on high for 5-7 minutes. Turn dish once during cooking time. Let stand (covered) for 5 minutes. For sauce, heat reserved sour cream mixture in microwave on medium power for 35 seconds. Pour warm sauce over fish, garnish with parsley sprigs and serve immediately.

Sweet And Sour Mahi Mahi

Serves: 4
Prep Time: 15-25 minutes

1	lb. mahi mahi fillets	2	T. brown sugar
	flour	1	tsp. soy sauce
2	T. butter	1/2	tsp. pepper
1/2	cup pineapple juice	1/4	cup vinegar
3	T. cooking oil		

Rinse mahi mahi and coat with flour. Melt butter in skillet and saute fillets for 5-7 minutes, turning once, until fish is flaky and tender. While fish is cooking, combine pineapple juice, oil, sugar, soy sauce, pepper and vinegar; heat until bubbly. When mahi mahi is cooked, pour sauce over fish and serve.

Meals Of The Midwest

Flat Fishing In The Midwest

Midwestern country has the most varied freshwater fishing in North America with the least varied habitat and not a mountain in sight! Because the Midwest has 99 percent of all the water in America stuffed into the Great Lakes and the biggest river in America, the mighty Mississippi, it's not very surprising that a greater percentage of the population here fish than anywhere else in the U.S. As a result, savvy states like Missouri and Michigan pay close attention to fisheries' matters (the former even has a special sales tax). Fish and game departments have, with judicious stocking, introduced salmon, steelhead, brown trout and exotic pike species.

Careful management keeps muskie fishermen, those compulsive types who seem even more willing than winter steelheaders to wait for action, in good spirits. Add pike, walleye, panfish, monster catfish and sturgeon to a recovering lake trout population with decent brown and rainbow trout fishing and it's easy to see why there are more fishing boats on the Great Lakes and Midwest impoundments and rivers than on any other waters in the country.

Ice Isn't Always Nice

Ice fishing is as basic to Midwestern life as rooting for the Green Bay Packers or Chicago Bears. Massive shanty towns and fancy angler creations mask the dangers discovered by Lewis Sweet in 1929 when he headed out to his shanty on Lake Michigan's Straits of Mackinac to dangle a decoy and, hopefully, spear a lake trout.

Sweet got his laker. Then winds rose, and ice broke away from shore. Since nobody should swim in frigid winter waters, Sweet was faced with a 60-mile, open lake and a rapidly shrinking ice floe.

Rescuers gathered after the storm blew out a day later. But Sweet and his shanty were gone. Four days of searching—but no Sweet. Friends walked the shore. The Coast Guard searched open water. Aircraft looked down into the broken flows. No Sweet.

Sweet, however, hadn't died. His diminishing ice prison drifted past the islands where Sweet expected to ground. Instead, as Sweet built ice walls to protect himself from arctic blasts, the shrinking floe piled up against While Shoals Light, a tiny pimple of a lighthouse on the body of Lake Michigan. Sweet chopped his way up a sheer stone face, but was turned back by freezing feet and exhaustion. So, still determined, he stacked ice chunks until he could mount the icy base and break into the lighthouse where food and shelter waited.

After eating, Sweet rested. With frozen fingers and toes thawing, he was unable to attract the last search planes.

Sweet waited. A cold north wind froze the lake. After a futile attempt to signal shore more than 12 miles away, he set out to stumble and crawl to land. It took two days and nights, but he made it (still dragging his trusty ax and the big laker he'd speared from his shanty). Fortunately, Midwestern fishing isn't quite as hazardous.

Midwest Glamour Fish

Muskies make anglers wonder exactly who's in charge. Swimmers who suddenly realize that the peeler core submerged near shore transmuted itself into a muskie lurking until dinner may hear the theme from "Jaws." Tales of muskies big enough to swallow children and dogs add spice to an angler's life. So do the fins of big spawning female pike.

Muskie and pike seem particularly able to melt anglers' brains and cause all sorts of odd behavior like the dubious basis of some long-held records. There's even an odd cross, the tiger muskie (a hybrid between pike and muskie that's popular with fish and game departments because it depletes overpopulations of panfish and won't reproduce). Consider the original pike north of 60 degrees latitude. You should realize that pike aren't exactly difficult to lure or bait, and it's no surprise that, as is the case with lakers and muskies, the best fishing is in Canada and in other remote waters.

Much of this is fly-in fishing. The mouth of the MacKenzie on Great Slave Lake and the wonderful waters south and west of Hudson Bay come to mind. Few of these are fished except around resorts and camps.

So fly-in and camp on your own—you'll be tossing back 15-pound fish and, if you pick the right water and get "last week's" conditions, you may cull fish below 20 pounds.

Group charter boats are a popular way of getting out into the deeper waters of the big lakes in the Midwest.

Steelhead And Salmon

When dead-alewife drifts two feet high stunk out tourists on the Michigan sand dunes it was time to do something. Lamprey eels had savaged lake trout populations that once controlled alewife numbers. The Great Lakes needed a predator; afterall, water quality was starting to come back. The Great Lakes looked to the West for predators and discovered salmon and steelhead.

Within a generation, fishing was reborn. Surf, shore and jetty anglers hooked fish. So many spawners jammed rivers that snagging was, unhappily, allowed by some states.

New methods like side planners and downriggers evolved. New lures and old systems, like noodle rods, evolved. The

cutting edge of trolling technology left saltwater and headed for the Great Lakes. Hundreds of marinas sheltered tens
of thousands of boats, and the best salmon fishery in the
world existed for a generation.

As baitfish numbers dropped back to sustainable levels,
salmon and steelhead action slowed somewhat. You can
make a case that Great Lakes salmon and steelhead are
the most successful introduction of fish into a body of water
since trout were stocked in New Zealand and Nepal.

Brown And Lake Trout

You might get an argument about the virtues of steelhead
and salmon from the flocks of brown trout addicts who
pitch lures from downtown riprap off Chicago, Traverse
City or Benton Harbor. Bringing in browns did seem odd.
North America has at least eight or nine different species
of trout and char of its own. But browns—whether the silver
Loch Levens for Scottish lakes that run to sea or still water
or the more colorful riverine "German browns"—remain
the favored fish of most. Both types do interbreed and col-
oration depends upon the season and habitat. They just
lost the "German" tag in World War I and World War II.

Browns came early. The first browns arrived in New York in
1883. The first 5,000 browns stocked in Michigan got
dumped from milk cans into the North Branch of the Per
Marquette River near Baldwin on April 11, 1884. Since
Loch Leven strains are basically a still-water fish, they
quickly moved into the lakes and spread into most tributary waters. Today, they'll hit off Chicago or in the Upper
Peninsula.

Where legal, the best fishing strategy for browns is to fish
after dark; they bite best when they can easily ambush
baitfish. It's also clear that browns can tolerate warmer
water better than other trout; thus, they are a good choice
for Midwestern reservoirs and clearwater streams.

Bass fishing isn't just a Southern pastime as this angler found on a Midwestern pond.

Lake trout seem rather overlooked in the thrust to catch steelhead, salmon and browns. Once the most abundant big fish in Great Lakes waters, they now seem almost an afterthought trolled up by the salmon and steelhead set. This is a shame because lakers come near the surface when the water cools and spawn, offering decent action. Lakers under eight pounds bake or smoke nicely, too.

'Eaters'

Some fish for glory. Some fish for food. Walleyes recently gained fame as a tournament fish, and they taste too good to release!

Second only to walleyes, and doubtless the most common-ly caught fish in the Midwest, yellow perch shine in the pan even though they don't exactly challenge tackle. (Pound-test line and ultra-light gear work best).

Cats!

Catfish seem the Rodney Dangerfield of fish. They get little respect, look rather odd and lumpy and, on consideration, offer delicious delights, The Midwest comes with a serious assortment. Blue catfish inhabit the Mississippi and its lower tributaries. Reports of 200-pound fish spiced Yankee credulity before the Civil War. Today 100 pounds is about tops and 20- to 30-pound fish offer a heavyweight chal-lenge for the heave-and-haul set.

Flathead catfish, the other heavyweight of the family, offer a challenge, especially on the Missouri and other larger waters where the current record was taken.

Channel catfish eat, fight and live in moving, clear water. Some hit flies or lures—all hit recently deceased minnows. You even hear tales of channel cats hitting poppers and bass bugs.

It seems likely that the best channel catfishing in the world is in Canada's Red River in southern Manitoba and in waters like the Nelson and Assiniboine around Lake Winnipeg.

Most of the rest of the family—white cats, bullheads and the like—get as little respect as sunnies, but fill the action needs of the small fry. All of these are delicious when filleted, and, since the invention of the electric knife, very easy to clean.

Sturgeon

At the big end of the Midwest size spectrum, lake sturgeon offer a unique challenge, wonderful eating and the makings of decent caviar. Given their size, most anglers enjoy accidental hook ups and "temporary custody only."

However, the current world record lake sturgeon was taken with a careful plan, so it can be done.

Accessibility

You can make a case that the reason the Midwest offers such a concentration of fishermen is geological. No place else in America, and in few places in the world, do you find so many shallow, productive lakes, so many decent streams and so much fishing without the dubious joys of high peaks, swamps and other access challenges. A few areas, like the wilderness waters around Ely, Minnesota, and, of course, Canada's vast shield of shallow lakes and productive waters, require an effort to access. Most do not.

Some anglers claim you can find good fishing via public transportation from any Midwestern city. Downtown browns in Chicago, yellow perch out of Green Bay, smallmouth and walleye near Detroit and cruising salmon and steelhead just about anywhere the water is deep and cold!

Adaptability

Even though specialists may, over a season, catch more

and bigger fish in their target species, opportunists have more fun. You should always come equipped for panfish, salmon, catfish, steelhead, muskies and walleyes! Nobody can catch fish when a given species has lockjaw or a given water looks like cocoa. Consider flies, lures and bait and switch to suit conditions. This is, after all, a fishing cookbook. Like the old Hungarian recipe for pheasant stew that starts, "first you poach a pheasant," you need fish to "make the grease sizzle."

America's Heartland: The Best Of The Midwest

Serves: 4-6

The Midwest offers flavors almost as diverse as the climate in St. Louis. Scandinavian fish dishes, a strong German and Italian presence and lots of English and Scottish specialties belie its undeserved reputation for bland food. Wonderful beer does well with these dishes, and you won't find better raw materials for fish recipes than walleye and yellow perch.

Salad: Tomato & Onion Salad With Vinaigrette Dressing

2	green onions
3	fresh tomatoes
1	small red onion

Vinaigrette Dressing:

1/4	cup olive oil
1	tsp. red wine vinegar
1	T. water
1	tsp. dry mustard
1	tsp. dried oregano leaves
1	tsp. freshly ground black pepper

In small bowl, combine dressing ingredients. On platter, slice green onions, tomatoes and red onion. Pour vinaigrette dressing over tomato salad and serve. (Note: Garden tomatoes and onions make this dish sing. If you don't garden, shop at a farm-fresh food stand. You may also use paper-thin slices of sweet Valdosta or Walla Walla onions.)

Entree: Broiled Walleye With Mustard Sauce

1 1/2	lbs. walleye fillets
4	T. butter
1/4	tsp. salt
1/8	tsp. pepper

Mustard Sauce:
- 1 T. butter
- 2 T. chopped shallots (or green onions)
- $^1/_2$ cup dry white wine
- 1 T. red wine vinegar
- $^1/_3$ cup Dijon Mustard
- $^3/_4$ cup heavy whipping cream
- $^1/_4$ cup sour cream

Rinse fillets and pat dry. Melt butter with salt and pepper. Brush fillets with seasoned butter and broil for 10-12 minutes or until fish flakes. Add mustard sauce before serving.

To make mustard sauce, combine butter and shallots in saucepan. Cook over medium heat until tender, about 6 minutes. Add wine and vinegar and cook until reduced by half. Add remaining ingredients and cook for 5 minutes or until sauce thickens. (Tip: Sauce can be made while fish is broiling.)

Dessert: Pear Pie

- 4 pears
- $^1/_3$ cup sugar
- $^1/_2$ cup walnuts
- $1^1/_2$ T. tapioca
- 1 T. lemon juice
- $^1/_4$ tsp. ground ginger
- 1 uncooked pie crust

Streusel Topping:
- 1 cup flour
- $^1/_2$ tsp. ground cinnamon
- $^1/_2$ cup brown sugar
- 1 stick softened butter

Preheat oven to 425 degrees. In large bowl, cut pears into 1-inch chunks. Add sugar, walnuts, tapioca, lemon juice and ginger. Spread pear mixture evenly into pie crust.

To make topping, combine flour, cinnamon and brown sugar in small bowl. Add butter and rub mixture through your fingers until small lumps appear. Sprinkle mixture over pears. Bake for

40 minutes or until crust is brown. Serve with vanilla ice cream.

Creamy Delight
Serves: 4-6

Portions don't always work out when you bake a big fish or cook a school of small ones. This lovely dish works with cooked left-over salmon, steelhead and other fish. Even fried leftovers are okay if you remove the skin. Crappie and yellow perch work well, too. Cook the fish when it's fresh, and freeze enough flaked fish for this dish. If you thaw the fish in the microwave, cut the potatoes into much smaller pieces and use a frozen pie shell. You can finish the entire meal in 30 minutes.

Entree: Creamed Salmon On Toast

2	cups cooked salmon, flaked
3	T. butter
3	T. flour
1^1/$_2$	cups milk
	salt and (white) pepper to taste
	paprika
8	bread slices, toasted and buttered

Melt butter in saucepan over medium heat. Remove from heat and blend in flour. Stir in ^{1}/$_2$ cup milk and mix well. Add remaining milk. Season with salt and pepper. Stir, bring to a near boil, reduce heat and simmer until sauce thickens. Add fish and simmer for 3 more minutes. Serve on hot buttered toast and sprinkle paprika over top. (Note: Leftover cooked shrimp or fish work great for this dish. Cooked shrimp or crayfish also make an attractive garnish.)

Side Dish No. 1: Potatoes With Tomato Sauce

3	medium potatoes
1	8-oz. can tomato sauce
1	tsp. oregano or basil leaves
2	tsp. dry parsley flakes
^{1}/$_4$	tsp. salt (optional)
^{1}/$_4$	tsp. pepper

Wash and peel potatoes, then cut into quarters. Spray baking pan with nonstick spray and arrange potatoes in single layer. Combine tomato sauce with oregano, parsley, salt and pepper. Pour sauce over potatoes and bake at 350 degrees for 45 minutes or until done.

Side Dish No. 2: Lemon Butter-Dill Brussels Sprouts

1	lb. brussels sprouts
3	T. melted butter
1	T. lemon juice
1/4	tsp. salt (optional)
1/4	tsp. pepper

Remove wilted outer leaves of brussels sprouts. Cut off small bit of stem end, then cut 1/8-inch cross in each stem. Wash brussels sprouts thoroughly. In skillet over medium heat, add brussels sprouts and cover with 1 1/2-inches water. Boil for 15 minutes or until desired doneness. Drain and place in serving bowl. Add melted butter, lemon juice, salt and pepper. Toss and serve.

Dessert: Applesauce Pie With Whipped Cream

1	graham cracker crust or conventional pie shell
2	cups homemade or bottled chunky applesauce
1/2	cup chopped walnuts
2	cups whipped cream

Prepare graham cracker pie shell according to package directions; cool. Put walnuts in bottom of pie shell. (Note: If using conventional pastry shell, lightly coat inside of shell with apricot jam to seal.) Add applesauce 3 hours before serving. Top pie with whipped cream and serve.

Hale And Hearty
Serves: 4

Colorful meals help appetites. Salmon, walleye or bass placed on a green bed and served with a cucumber salad, hot French cheese rolls and, if you like, a baked potato makes a grand meal. If you leave room for the oatmeal orange chocolate chip cookies, this mid-American delight will be the talk of the town!

Appetizer: Hot French Bread Cheese Rolls

4	6-inch-long French Bread rolls (split)
1	cup Parmesan Cheese
1	cup mayonnaise
1	cup green onions, finely chopped
	paprika

Preheat oven to 350 degrees. Combine cheese, mayonnaise and green onions; spread on split French rolls. Sprinkle paprika over bread. Broil until bubbly.

Salad: Cucumber Salad

2	cucumbers, sliced
$1/2$	red bell pepper, seeded and sliced
$1/2$	cup cilantro, chopped
1	small red onion, sliced

Dressing:

3	T. olive oil
1	T. lemon juice
2	T. red wine or malt vinegar
	salt and pepper to taste.

Mix salad ingredients in small bowl. Combine salad dressing ingredients and pour over salad. Season with salt and pepper.

Entree: Red Fish On A Green Bed

$1^1/2$	lbs. fish, whole, fillets or steaks
5	T. butter or margarine
1	pkg. frozen chopped spinach
$1/2$	cup heavy cream
2	T. lemon juice
1	tsp. tarragon leaves
$1/2$	tsp. salt
$1/4$	tsp. white pepper

Preheat oven to 350 degrees. Rinse fish and pat dry. Grease baking dish with 1 T. butter or margarine. Cook spinach according to package directions; drain and squeeze dry in towel. Combine spinach, cream, lemon juice, tarragon, salt and pepper; mix. Spread mixture in baking dish, top with fish and dot with remaining butter. Bake for 15-20 minutes or until fish flakes when tested with fork. Serve with lemon wedges and boiled red parsley potatoes.

Dessert: Oatmeal Orange Chocolate Chip Cookies

2	cups flour	2	eggs
1	tsp. baking soda		juice and grated rind from 1 orange
1	tsp. salt		
1	cup butter	2	cups quick oats
1	cup white sugar	1	cup chocolate chips
1	cup brown sugar, firmly packed	1	cup nuts (your choice)

Preheat oven to 375 degrees. Sift flour, soda and salt together; set aside. Cream butter and gradually add both sugars. Blend in unbeaten eggs and orange juice and beat well. Fold in flour mixture. Stir in oats, chocolate chips, nuts and grated orange peel. Drop teaspoonfuls of batter on greased cookie sheet. Bake for 9-12 minutes. (Makes 8 dozen cookies.)

Plain And Simple Fish
Serves: 4-6

Start with a classic fish and potato soup to warm up. Move to a tangy baked fish served with the delightful flavors of lemon-parsley rice and brandy dill carrots and end with a Midwest white cake with walnut frosting. This menu suits winter and summer, and you can use almost any fish in the soup and oven.

Soup: Fish & Potato Soup

$1/2$	lb. lean fish (bluegills, crappie, bass)	$1/4$	cup fresh parsley, chopped

2	medium potatoes	6	cups water
4	T. olive oil	4	eggs
2	T. butter	$^1/_8$	tsp. salt
2	garlic cloves, minced	$^1/_4$	tsp. pepper

Cut fish into 1-inch cubes. Cut potatoes into $^1/_2$-inch cubes. In saucepan, heat oil and butter over medium heat. Add garlic, parsley, water and potatoes. Cook for 10 minutes, then add fish and cook for 10 more minutes. Break whole eggs into soup mixture one at a time and cook until eggs are done (about 10 minutes). Add salt and pepper.

Entree: Tangy Baked Fillets

$1^1/_2$	lbs. fillets (yellow perch, sole, crappie)
1	tsp. butter or margarine
	salt and pepper
1	cup plain yogurt
1	garlic clove, minced
2	green onions, chopped
1	tsp. paprika (try Hot Hungarian!)
1	tsp. dillweed
1	lemon, thinly sliced.

Preheat oven to 350 degrees. Rinse and pat fish dry. Butter shallow baking dish and arrange fillets in single layer. Season with salt and pepper to taste. Combine remaining ingredients (except lemon) and spread over fish. Top each fillet with lemon slices and bake for 20 minutes or until fish flakes.

Side Dish No. 1: Lemon-Parsley Rice

2	cups water or chicken stock
1	cup raw rice
3	T. butter or margarine
	rind and juice from 1 lemon
$^1/_2$	cup chopped parsley

In saucepan, bring water to a boil. Add rice, cover and lower heat; simmer for 20 minutes. When rice is finished, fluff with fork and add remaining ingredients. Stir and serve.

Side Dish No. 2: Brandy Dilled Carrots

4   large carrots, peeled and sliced
1   T. butter
1   tsp. dillweed
2   T. brandy

In saucepan, cook carrots in barely enough water to cover for 5-10 minutes or until soft. Drain water and add butter and dill-weed. When butter melts, add brandy. As brandy evaporates, ignite with flame as you shake pan (use extreme caution). Serve immediately.

Dessert: White Cake With Chocolate Pudding Frosting

1/2   cup softened butter
2   eggs
3/4   cup sugar
1 3/4   cups all-purpose or cake flour
2   tsp. baking powder
1/4   tsp. salt
1/2   cup milk
1   tsp. vanilla extract

Frosting:
1   large can evaporated milk
1   stick butter
3/4   cup sugar
2   T. flour
3   egg yolks, slightly beaten
1   cup unsweetened chocolate chips
1/2   tsp. vanilla extract
1/2   cup chopped walnuts

Grease and flour two 8-inch layer baking pans. Preheat oven to 375 degrees. In mixing bowl, cream butter until light. Add eggs and continue to beat until thick and light. Add sugar, beating until light and creamy. On waxed paper, sift flour with baking powder and salt. Add flour mixture alternately with milk in thirds to butter mixture. Continue to beat after each addition. Stir in vanilla. Pour batter into prepared baking pans and bake for 20-25 minutes or until done. Remove from heat and cool on wire racks for about 5 minutes. Remove cakes from pans and let cool. To make frosting, combine milk, butter, sugar, flour and egg yolks in saucepan; cook until thick like pudding. Stir in chocolate chips and vanilla. Continue to cook over low heat until chips melt. Stir in walnuts and cool. Frost cold cakes and serve.

International Fish
Serves: 4-6

Because the Midwest is such a melting pot, this menu salutes cultural diversity with a French soup, a German entree, Hungarian potato pancakes and an Austrian dessert.

Appetizer: Seafood Bisque

1/2	lb. cooked crab, flaked
1/2	lb. cooked fish, flaked
1/2	lb. cooked shrimp, shelled
6	T. butter or margarine
1	medium onion, finely chopped
1	carrot, finely chopped
2	celery stalks, finely chopped
2	T. parsley, fresh or dried
1	7 1/2-oz. can clams, chopped or minced
3	cups clam juice
1/2	cup dry white wine
1/2	tsp. thyme leaves
1/2	tsp. dillweed
3	T. flour
1/4	tsp. salt
1/4	tsp. white pepper

Melt 3 T. butter in skillet over medium heat. Add onion, carrot, celery and parsley; saute until soft. Combine crab, fish, shrimp, canned clams with liquid plus clam juice, wine, thyme and dillweed. Bring to boil. Reduce heat to medium and cook for 5 minutes. Mix flour and remaining butter and roll into ball. (French cooks call this a roux). Divide seafood mixture. Add butter ball to half and stir over medium heat until sauce thickens. Season with salt and pepper. Blend remaining half of mixture for 3-5 seconds in blender. Combine mixtures and heat to serving temperature.

Entree: Fish In Beer

3	lbs. boned fish (pike or carp), skinned
2	cups water
1	bottle dark beer

1/2 cup parsley, chopped
1 medium onion, chopped
1 tsp. pickling spice
2 tsp. butter
3 T. cornstarch
1/4 cup water
2 tsp. lemon juice

Cut fish into serving-sized pieces. Combine water, beer, parsley, onion and pickling spice in skillet; bring to a near boil. Add fish and poach for 5 minutes or until fish flakes. With slotted spoon, remove fish to heated platter and add butter. Combine cornstarch and water and add to skillet. Boil and stir constantly until thickened. Add lemon juice. (You can adjust sweet-to-sour ratio with a little sugar if you like; it varies by beer and onion choices.) Pass fish and sauce separately.

Side Dish: Hungarian Potato Cakes

2 lbs. large potatoes, peeled
1 medium onion, peeled
2 eggs
2 T. flour
  salt and pepper to taste
1 tsp. paprika (try hot Hungarian!)
  cooking oil

In bowl, grate and combine potatoes and onion; add eggs, flour, salt and pepper and paprika. Heat oil over medium-high heat in skillet. Make pancakes with heaping teaspoonfuls of mix and brown on both sides. Remove to covered hot plate or oven until all are done. (Yields 30-40 pancakes.) Leftovers are great! (Tip: Applesauce made from coarsely chopped green, yellow and red apples complements this dish. It can be served for breakfast with sour cream and powdered sugar to help get ice fishermen up for the day!)

Dessert: Strawberry Pie

2 small boxes fresh strawberries
3/4 cup sugar
1 1/2 T. cornstarch

1   tsp. strawberry liqueur or brandy
1¹/₂ T. lemon juice
1   9-inch cooked pie shell, cooled
     whipped cream or ice cream

Clean whole strawberries; set aside one box. In saucepan, slice strawberries from remaining box and add sugar, cornstarch and liqueur. Cook over medium heat until thick and clear. Mash strawberries, if needed (mixture should look like jam). Cool, then stir in lemon juice. Place half of cooked strawberry mixture in pie shell. Arrange whole strawberries from other box in pie. Add remaining cooked strawberries and refrigerate for 2-3 hours. Top with whipped cream or vanilla ice cream.

Canadian Culinary Specialities
Serves: 6

Canadians, like the English, suffer a "bum rap" as cooks. Both countries offer wonderful food if you know how to ask for their specialities. These recipes came from Quebec, the most European of North America's cities. The entree works nicely with black, white or striped bass, salmon or steelhead and wall-eye. Like most recipes, it cooks a lot easier than it reads.

Salad: Spinach Salad With Burgundy Dressing

1   bunch spinach
1   cup sliced mushrooms
3   green onions, sliced
¹/₄ cup sliced almonds

Burgundy Dressing:
1   garlic clove, finely minced
¹/₄ tsp. salt
¹/₂ cup olive oil
3   T. red wine vinegar
¹/₄ cup catsup
¹/₂ tsp. Worcestershire sauce
¹/₂ tsp. dry mustard
1   raw egg (optional)
3   T. burgundy

In salad bowl, tear spinach into bite-sized pieces. Add mush-rooms, onions and almonds; mix well. To make dressing, com-bine all ingredients in small bowl. Refrigerate for 30 minutes. Serve with spinach salad when cold. (Note: If you have leftover cold roasted chicken or game birds such as dove, pheasants or quail, pick meat off the bones and sprinkle it on this salad and serve as a light lunch entree.)

Entree: French-Canadian Fish

1	3-lb. fish (whole), scaled and cleaned
2	medium onions, sliced.
1/4	cup bread crumbs
2	T. milk
4	T. butter
2	garlic cloves, minced
2	T. fresh parsley, chopped
2	tsp. fresh marjoram
1	tsp. grated lemon rind
2	egg yolks, beaten (use whites for potato recipe)
	salt and pepper to taste
1/2	cup white wine
1/2	cup vermouth
4	T. heavy cream
	dillweed

Pat fish dry with paper towel. In saucepan add onions and enough water to cover. Cook over medium heat for 5 minutes. Drain and press onions lightly to remove water. In small bowl, combine bread crumbs with milk. Soak for 3 minutes; then squeeze dry. In skillet, melt 3 T. butter over medium heat. Add garlic and cook until soft. Stir in bread crumbs and add parsley, marjoram, lemon rind, egg yolks and salt and pepper. Cook for 2 minutes; cool.

Grease large, shallow ovenproof pan and add fish stuffed with bread crumb mixture. Spread drained onions around fish. Dot with remaining butter. Combine wine and vermouth; pour over fish. Cover pan with lid or aluminum foil. Bake for 40-50 minutes at 325 degrees or until fish flakes when tested with fork. Remove onions with slotted spoon to platter, making a bed for cooked fish. Place fish on center of onions and keep warm in oven. Reduce remaining liquid over high heat until syrupy consistency. Stir in cream and cook until thickened. Pour cream sauce over fish, top with dill weed and serve.

Side Dish: Creamy Red Potato Mash

10-12 small red potatoes, unpeeled
- **$1/2$ cup heavy cream**
- **2 egg whites**
- **4 T. butter**
- **3 T. grated Parmesan or Romano cheese**
- **$1/2$ tsp. salt**
- **$1/8$ tsp. pepper**
- **$1/2$ cup milk**

Wash and scrub potatoes; then cut into quarters. (If potatoes are larger than tennis balls, cut into 8 pieces.) In saucepan, add potatoes and enough water to cover. Cook over medium heat until tender (about 15 minutes); drain. Whip cream and egg whites in separate bowls. Butter 9-inch-wide baking pan. Add 3 T. butter, cheese, salt and pepper to potatoes; mash. Stir in milk and mix well. Fold in whipped cream and egg whites. Turn entire mixture into baking pan. Dot with remaining butter. Bake for 10 minutes at 325 degrees.

Dessert: Sour Cream Chocolate Cake With Cream Cheese

- **2 cups sugar**
- **2 T. shortening**
- **2 T. butter**
- **$1/2$ cup cocoa**
- **$1/2$ cup sour milk (add a splash of vinegar)**
- **1 cup boiling water**
- **2 eggs**
- **1 tsp. vanilla**
- **$1^1/2$ tsp. baking soda**
- **$1/8$ tsp. salt**
- **2 cups sifted cake flour**

Cream Cheese Frosting:
  1   **8-oz. pkg. cream cheese, softened**
  2   **squares unsweetened chocolate**
2¹/₂   **T. milk**
  ³/₄   **cup powdered sugar**
  6   **T. butter, melted**
  1   **cup chopped nuts**

In mixer, cream sugar with shortening and butter. Add cocoa, milk and boiling water. Blend well. Add eggs, vanilla, baking soda, salt and flour; mix well. Pour batter into two buttered and floured 8-inch cake pans. Bake for 30 minutes or until done. Cool for 10 minutes on racks before removing cake from pan.

In mixer, beat cream cheese until light and fluffy. In saucepan over low heat (or in microwave), melt chocolate in milk. Remove from heat, stir and add to cream cheese. Add powdered sugar and melted butter; stir until well-blended. Cool. Frost cake. Cover sides or top (not both) with chopped nuts—pecans, walnuts and macadamia nuts work well. Best served cold; store in refrigerator. (In Hungary well-mannered guests ask the hostess about dessert before dinner so they can leave room for the especially rich Eastern European desserts. You may want to make this cake only when you have 8-10 for dinner.)

Recipes For:

Mollusks

Mullet

Pike

Perch

Pollock

Pompano

Rockfish

Roughy

Salmon

Shark

Smelt

Snapper

Sole

Abalone Balls

Serves: 20
Prep Time: 30 minutes

2	abalone, ground	2	cups seasoned
2	eggs		bread crumbs
6	jalapeno peppers, diced	2	cups flour
2	green onions, diced	2	cups cornmeal
1^1/$_2$-2	cups cheddar cheese	3-4	cups cooking oil

Combine abalone, eggs, peppers, onions, cheese and bread crumbs; mix well. Roll mixture into walnut-sized balls in flour and cornmeal. Deep-fry for 2^1/$_2$-3 minutes in hot oil. Drain on paper towel and serve.

Bernard Hardesty
Chico, California

Deep-Fried Calamari

Serves: 6
Prep Time: 30-40 minutes

1	lb. squid, cut into 1/2-3/4-inch slices	1	bottle tartar sauce
2	cups whole milk	1	bottle shrimp cocktail sauce
	flour		lemon wedges
	cornmeal		
1	qt. sunflower or safflower cooking oil		

Saturate squid in milk. (Use whole milk because it bonds coating better.) Roll squid strips in equal parts of flour and cornmeal to coat. In frying pan or deep-fat fryer, heat oil without smoking. Gradually add pieces of squid to hot oil. Cook for approximately 2 minutes or until squid is almost golden brown. Remove from oil with slotted spoon. Drain on paper towel and serve with tartar sauce, cocktail sauce and lemon wedges.

Continental Clam & Corn Chowder

Serves: 6
Prep Time: 45-50 minutes

24	clams, shucked and chopped
4	bacon slices, chopped
1	cup onion, minced
2	cups potatoes, diced
1	cup clam juice or water
2	celery stalks, chopped
1 1/2	cups canned corn
3	cups milk
1/4	tsp. Worcestershire sauce
3	T. flour
2	T. butter
1	tsp. salt
1/4	tsp. pepper

In large saucepan, fry bacon until crisp. Add onion and cook until tender. Add potatoes and clam juice; cover and simmer for 20 minutes or until potatoes are tender. Add celery, corn, milk and Worcestershire sauce. Blend flour and butter together; add to mixture and stir. Cook for 5 minutes or until chowder is thoroughly heated and slightly thickened, stirring frequently. Add salt and pepper and serve.

Chesapeake Clams Appetizer

Serves: several (yields 24 appetizers)
Prep Time: 30-35 minutes

24	clams, steamed and chopped	1/4	cup parsley, chopped
24	clam shells, scrubbed and cleaned	3	T. onion, chopped
1	cup dry bread crumbs	1	tsp. oregano
3/4	cup Parmesan cheese, grated	1/2	tsp. garlic salt
		2	T. oil
		24	small bacon squares paprika to taste

Divide chopped clams among shells. Combine bread crumbs, Parmesan cheese, parsley, onion, oregano, garlic salt and oil. Spread crumb mixture over chopped clams (1 tsp. per shell). Place one bacon square on each shell. Bake at 350 degrees until bacon is crisp. Sprinkle paprika on top and serve hot.

Curried Clam Sauce For Pasta

Serves: 4-6
Prep Time: 20-25 minutes

24-36	clams, cleaned	2	tsp. curry powder
1	cup dry white wine		your favorite prepared pasta
2	bay leaves		
3	T. oil	1/4	cup fresh parsley, minced
4	garlic cloves, chopped		
1/4	tsp. salt		
1/4	tsp. ground pepper		

Place clams in large saucepan; add wine and bay leaves. Steam for 3-5 minutes until clams open. (Discard clams that do not open.) Remove flesh from shells. Strain broth and set aside. Heat oil and saute garlic until cooked but not browned. Add reserved broth to oil; add salt and pepper. Bring to a boil, simmering for 5 minutes. Add clams and curry to broth, stirring well. Pour over hot, cooked pasta and sprinkle parsley on top.

Key Conch Chowder

Serves: 8
Prep Time: 40-45 minutes

1 **lb. conch meat, prepared and sliced**	2 **cups potatoes, diced**
1 **T. butter**	3 **cups canned tomatoes**
1 **onion, chopped**	1 **cup carrots, diced**
3 **T. flour**	2 **bay leaves**
3 **cups water**	1/4 **cup catsup**

In large saucepan, melt butter and saute onion until tender. Stir in flour and gradually add water. Add potatoes, tomatoes, carrots, bay leaves and catsup. Cover and simmer until potatoes are cooked yet firm. Add conch meat and simmer for 6-8 minutes.

Bay Island Fritters

Serves: several (yields 25 fritters)
Prep Time: 25-40 minutes

1/2 **lb. conch meat, prepared and ground**	1/2 **tsp. garlic powder**
1/2 **cup tomatoes, peeled, seeded and chopped**	1 **cup milk**
1/4 **cup green pepper, minced**	1/2 **tsp. baking powder**
3/4 **cup onion, minced**	1/2 **tsp. salt**
1 **tsp. Worcestershire sauce**	1/2 **tsp. pepper**
	2 **cups all-purpose flour**
	cook oil for frying

Combine first 7 ingredients together; mix. Sift baking powder, salt, pepper and flour together; mix thoroughly. Gradually stir flour mixture into conch mixture. In deep-fat fryer, heat oil to 375 degrees. Spoon batter by tablespoons into hot oil. Cook for approximately 3 minutes or until golden brown, turning once. Drain on paper towel. Keep fritters warm in slow oven until all are ready to serve.

Mussel Sauce With Pasta

Serves: 6
Prep Time: 40-55 minutes

- **1 lb. mussels, shelled and chopped**
- **6 tomatoes, peeled, seeded and chopped**
- **2 T. parsley, chopped**
- **1 tsp. dried basil**
- **1 tsp. oregano**
- **2 T. lemon juice**
- **2 garlic cloves, minced**
- **1 tsp. dried red pepper flakes**
- **1 lb. linguini or other pasta**
-    **Parmesan cheese, grated**

Combine tomatoes, parsley, basil, oregano, lemon juice, garlic, pepper flakes and mussels in saucepan. Bring to a boil. Reduce heat and simmer (uncovered) for 15-20 minutes, stirring occasionally. Cook pasta according to package directions and drain. Toss pasta with half of sauce and divide among 6 deep plates; top with remaining sauce and Parmesan cheese.

'Mussel' In On The Stew

- **1 pt. mussels, steamed and shucked**
- **4 T. butter**
- **$1/2$ tsp. onion, grated**
- **$1^1/2$ cups milk**
- **$1/2$ cup cream**
- **$1/2$ tsp. salt**
- **$1/8$ tsp. pepper**
- **2 T. parsley, chopped**

Melt butter in top of double boiler and lightly saute onion. Add mussels, milk, cream, salt and pepper. When milk is hot and mussels float, add parsley and serve.

Vinaigrette Style Mussels With Sauce

Serves: 6
Prep Time: 40-55 minutes

- **4 lbs. mussels, cleaned, soaked and debearded**
- **1 cup dry white wine**
- **2 garlic cloves, chopped**
- **1 bay leaf**
- **1 small onion, chopped**

Vinaigrette Sauce:
- **1/2 cup wine vinegar**
- **2 T. Dijon mustard**
- **3/4 cup olive oil**
- **2 garlic cloves, chopped**
- **1/4 tsp. salt**
- **fresh black pepper to taste**
- **1 small hot pepper, chopped**
- **1 medium red bell pepper, chopped**
- **1 green bell pepper, chopped**
- **1/2 cup shallots, minced**
- **2 T. fresh parsley, minced**

In large saucepan, add mussels to wine, garlic, bay leaf and onion. Bring liquid to a boil and steam mussels for about 3 minutes until they open. Remove mussels with slotted spoon, discarding unopened mussels. When cool, shuck mussels and place in large serving dish; set aside. To prepare vinaigrette sauce, combine vinegar, mustard, olive oil, garlic, salt and pepper in large sealable jar; close jar and shake vigorously to blend. Add remaining ingredients to jar, stirring peppers into liquid. Pour sauce over mussels and serve at room temperature.

Traditional Oysters Rockefeller

Serves: 6
Prep Time: 30-45 minutes

36	oysters on the half shell	2	T. bacon bits
2	cups spinach, cooked	1	T. parsley, chopped
1/4	cup onion, chopped	1	tsp. salt
1/2	cup dry bread crumbs	6	drops hot pepper
6	T. butter, melted		sauce

In food processor, blend spinach, onion, bread crumbs, bacon bits, parsley, salt and hot pepper sauce. Stir in melted butter. In shallow baking pan, arrange oysters. Spread mixture over oysters and bake at 400 degrees for 10 minutes. Place briefly under broiler to brown.

Easy Baked Oysters

Serves: 4-6
Prep Time: 30-45 minutes

24	fresh oysters, shucked
6	T. butter
1	cup fresh bread crumbs
1	garlic clove, chopped
2	T. fresh parsley, minced
1/3	cup Parmesan cheese

Generously butter oblong baking dish. Melt 2 T. butter in skillet. Add bread crumbs and garlic and saute until golden brown. Stir in parsley. Spread 2/3 cup of crumb mixture in bottom of baking dish and arrange oysters on top in single layer. Add Parmesan cheese to remaining bread crumbs and spread over top of oysters. Dot with remaining butter. Bake at 450 degrees on middle shelf of oven for 12-15 minutes or until juices bubble. Serve immediately.

Micro-Easy Oyster Saute

Serves: 6
Prep Time: 40-55 minutes

1^1/$_2$	**lbs. oysters**
2	**T. butter**
^{1}/$_2$	**cup white wine**
2	**cups mushrooms, sliced**
^{1}/$_2$	**cup green onions, chopped**
^{1}/$_2$	**cup bell pepper, chopped**
^{1}/$_3$	**cup celery, chopped**
1	**tsp. dill**
3	**T. fresh parsley, minced**
2	**T. lemon juice**

In 9-inch baking dish, melt butter. Add wine, mushrooms, green onions, bell pepper and celery. Cover and microwave on medium for 3 minutes or until slightly tender. Add oysters and dill; cover and microwave an additional 8-10 minutes on medium setting or until oysters are opaque. Uncover and sprinkle parsley and lemon juice over top.

7 Seas Stuffed Peppers

Serves: 6
Prep Time: 40-50 minutes

1	**lb. fresh scallops**
2	**medium red, yellow and green bell peppers (with tops, seeds and membranes removed)**
1	**tsp. oil**
1¹/₂	**cups fresh mushrooms, sliced**
¹/₄	**cup green onions, finely chopped**
³/₄	**lb. medium-sized fresh shrimp, peeled and deveined**
1	**T. lemon juice**
1	**tsp. dried, whole dillweed**
	dash hot sauce
	pinch pepper
6	**soda crackers (unsalted), crushed**

Boil prepared peppers for 5 minutes; drain and set aside. In large skillet, add oil and heat until hot. Add mushrooms and green onions, sauteeing until tender. Add shrimp, scallops, lemon juice, dillweed, hot sauce and pepper. Cook over medium heat for 3-4 minutes, stirring constantly. Reduce heat and add cracker crumbs, stirring until thickened. Spoon mixture into peppers and serve immediately.

Micro-Easy Coquille St. Jacques

Serves: 4
Prep Time: 40-50 minutes

1	**lb. scallops**
1	**cup white wine**
3/4	**cup water**
1	**T. lemon juice**
1	**bay leaf**
1	**T. parsley, chopped**
1/4	**lb. mushrooms, chopped**
6	**T. butter**
4	**T. flour**
2	**egg yolks**
4	**T. heavy cream**
	bread crumbs
	parsley sprigs
	paprika

In 3-qt. casserole, combine wine, water, lemon juice, bay leaf
and parsley. Cover and microwave on high for 3 minutes. Add
scallops and mushrooms; cover and cook for 6 minutes on medium-high, stirring once. Remove bay leaf and drain, reserving
1 3/4 cups broth. In small bowl, melt 4 T. butter; stir in flour and
reserved broth. Mix thoroughly. Microwave for 3-4 minutes until
thick and smooth. Blend egg yolks and cream together; add to
sauce. Stir and cook for 2-3 minutes. (Do not overcook.) Place
scallops and mushrooms into cleaned shells or layer in shallow
baking dish. Spoon cream sauce over scallops, sprinkle bread
crumbs on top and dot with remaining butter. Microwave on
high for 2 minutes. Garnish with additional chopped parsley and
paprika. Serve immediately. (If desired, scallops may be baked
in oven at 400 degrees for 10 minutes to brown bread crumbs,
omitting last 2 minutes in microwave.)

Mediterranean Stuffed Squid

Serves: 4-6
Prep Time: 1 hour, 20 minutes

1	lb. squid tails, cleaned and intact
3/4	cup mozzarella cheese, grated
2	T. parsley, chopped
1	tsp. dried oregano
1	tsp. dried basil
1/3	cup Parmesan cheese
1/2	cup bread crumbs
1/3	cup onions, finely chopped
1	cup mushrooms, chopped
1/4	cup olive oil
1/4	cup tomato sauce
1/2	cup white wine
1/2	cup water
1/4	cup parsley, chopped
	dry bread crumbs

To make stuffing, combine mozzarella cheese, parsley, oregano, basil, Parmesan cheese, bread crumbs, onions and mushrooms. Stuff mixture into squid tails until plump but not packed. Close and secure openings with toothpicks. Arrange stuffed squid in single layer in greased baking dish. In separate bowl, combine olive oil, tomato sauce, wine, water and parsley. Pour mixture over squid; top with heavy coating of bread crumbs. Bake at 350 degrees for 30-60 minutes or until squid is tender.

Fried Squid Rings

Serves: 4
Prep Time: 20-30 minutes

3 lbs. squid
cooking oil
1 can beer (room temperature)
1 cup flour
1 tsp. salt
1 tsp. paprika

Heat oil to 375 degrees. Combine beer, flour, salt and paprika in large bowl. Dip squid rings into batter, letting excess batter run off. Drop squid rings into hot oil. Brown a few rings at a time on both sides and remove. (Squid will stay crisp in baking pan lined with paper towels.)

Italian Mullet Soup

Serves: (yields 7 cups)
Prep Time: 20-30 minutes

1¹/₂	**lbs. mullet fillets, cut into ¹/₂-inch pieces**
³/₄	**cup onion, chopped**
2	**garlic cloves, minced**
1	**T. oil**
1	**T. sugar**
1	**8-oz. can tomato sauce**
1	**28-oz. can stewed tomatoes**
¹/₂	**cup white wine**
1¹/₂	**T. dried Italian seasoning**
2	**bay leaves**
	salt and pepper to taste
1	**T. parsley, chopped**

In large saucepan, saute onion and garlic in oil until tender. Add sugar, tomato sauce, tomatoes, wine, Italian seasoning, bay leaves, salt and pepper. Add fish and cook for 10 minutes or until fish is tender. Sprinkle parsley over top and serve.

Mullet A La Palm Beach

Serves: 4
Prep Time: 15-20 minutes

1	**lb. mullet fillets**
¹/₄	**cup flour**
2	**T. butter**
1	**orange, sectioned**
1	**grapefruit, sectioned**

Dredge mullet in flour and saute in butter for 5-7 minutes or until fish is flaky and tender, turning once. Alternate orange and grapefruit sections over fillets and pour pan drippings over fruit. Heat fish under broiler for 15-20 seconds to warm fruit.

Micro-Easy Mullet Magic

Serves: 6
Prep Time: 40-45 minutes

2-3	**lbs. mullet fillets**
2	**T. grated orange rind**
1/4	**cup onion, chopped**
1/2	**cup celery, diced**
4	**T. margarine**
1	**cup orange juice**
2	**T. lemon juice**
1/2	**cup water (or mandarin orange juice)**
1/4	**tsp. salt**
1 1/2	**cups instant rice, uncooked**
1	**3-oz. can mandarin oranges, drained**
1/4	**cup slivered almonds (optional)**
	paprika (optional)
	orange wheels (optional)

In deep glass bowl, combine orange rind, onion, celery and margarine. Cover and microwave for 2 minutes on high. Add orange and lemon juice, water and salt. Cover and microwave on high for 6-7 minutes or until mixture boils. Remove and stir in rice; cover and let stand for 5 minutes. Add mandarin oranges. Spoon rice mixture into buttered oblong baking dish. Place fillets over rice and cover with vented plastic wrap. Microwave on high for 10-11 minutes or until fish flakes easily when tested with fork. Remove and let stand (covered) for 5 minutes. Sprinkle almond slices and paprika on top. Garnish with orange wheels, if desired.

Lemon-Garlic Perch

Serves: 4
Prep Time: 1 hour, 10-20 minutes

- **1 lb. ocean perch fillets**
- **1 lemon (juice and grated rind)**
- **1 T. brown sugar**
- **1/2 T. garlic powder**
- **1 T. oil**

Combine grated lemon peel, juice, sugar, garlic powder and oil. Place single layer of fillets in lemon marinade. Marinate in refrigerator for 1 hour, turning once. Place marinated fish on lightly oiled broiler pan and baste with marinade. Broil 4-5 inches from heat, basting occasionally, for 5-7 minutes or until fish is flaky and tender.

A 'Dilly' Of A Perch

Serves: 6
Prep Time: 35-40 minutes

- **2 lbs. ocean perch**
- **6 T. butter, melted**
- **1 tsp. salt**
- **1/4 tsp. pepper**
- **1/2 cup lime juice**
- **1/2 tsp. dried dill**
- **1 lime, thinly sliced**
- **1/4 cup parsley, chopped**

Pour melted butter into oblong baking dish; add perch. Sprinkle salt, pepper and lime juice over fish. Bake fish at 350 degrees for 20 minutes, basting occasionally. Sprinkle dill over fish and top with lime slices. Bake an additional 5 minutes or until fish is flaky and tender. Sprinkle parsley over top and serve.

Perch-Stuffed Artichokes

Serves: 4
Prep Time: 50-60 minutes

1-1¹/₂ lbs. perch, cooked and flaked
   4   small artichokes
  ¹/₂   sweet red pepper, chopped
¹/₂-³/₄ cup dry bread crumbs
   ¹/₃   cup mozzarella cheese, shredded
   ¹/₂   tsp. dried oregano
    1   medium lemon, halved
   ¹/₄   cup butter, melted
    2   cups water

Cut stems 1-inch from tops of artichokes. With scissors, snip tips
from leaves. In large pot of boiling water, cook artichokes for 20
minutes. Remove with slotted spoon and drain upside down on
paper towels. When cool enough to handle, remove and discard
center leaves and choke. In medium-sized bowl, combine fish,
peppers, bread crumbs, cheese, oregano and juice squeezed
from half of lemon to form filling. (Add 1-2 T. water if still too
dry.) Add filling to artichoke leaves and centers, placing small
amounts in outer leaves. Put leaves into 8-inch casserole and
add water and juice from other half of lemon. Set artichokes
upright in casserole. Drizzle butter over each artichoke. Cover
tightly with foil and bake at 400 degrees for 15 minutes until fil-
ing is heated and leaves can be easily removed. Cover and let
stand for 10 minutes. Spoon pan juices over artichokes before
serving if desired.

Northern Pike

Serves: 4-6
Prep Time: 25-40 minutes

**3-5 lbs. fish, skinned and
cut into large chunks**
3 qts. water
1/2 cup sugar
2 T. vinegar
1 medium onion (whole)

2 bay leaves
1 celery stalk, chopped
2 tsp. red pepper
2 T. salt
3 tsp. black pepper

In 6-qt. kettle, combine all ingredients (except fish) and bring to boil. Add fish and boil for 10-15 minutes until fish separates from large bones. Serve immediately with melted butter.

David Glossenger
Honesdale, Pennsylvania

Quick Bake Pollock

Serves: 4
Prep Time: 20-25 minutes

1 **lb. pollock fillets**	1/4 **tsp. onion powder**
1 **T. butter**	1/2 **tsp. basil**
1/3 **cup bread crumbs**	1/4 **tsp. paprika**
1/4 **tsp. garlic powder**	1 **T. lemon juice**

Coat pollock fillets with melted butter. Combine bread crumbs, garlic and onion powder, basil and paprika; dredge fillets in breading. Place fish in baking dish and drizzle with lemon juice. Bake at 400 degrees for 10-15 minutes or until fish is flaky and tender.

Micro-Easy Pollock Italian Style

Serves: 4-6
Prep Time: 20-25 minutes

1-11/2 **lbs. pollock fillets**
  1 **16-oz. jar prepared Italian spaghetti sauce**
1/2 **cup Parmesan cheese**
   angel hair pasta or very thin spaghetti
  2 **T. fresh parsley, minced**

Spread 2 T. spaghetti sauce on each fillet and roll up jelly-roll style. Secure ends with toothpicks and place rollups in non-metallic, shallow baking dish. Pour remaining sauce over fish and sprinkle Parmesan cheese over top. Cover with plastic wrap and microwave on high for 8-10 minutes, rotating dish twice during cooking. Fish is done when center flakes easily when tested with fork. Let stand for 3 minutes (covered). Cook spaghetti and transfer to large serving platter. Arrange rollups on pasta, spooning sauce over both. Sprinkle parsley over top before serving.

Grand Strand Fish Cakes

Serves: 4
Prep Time: 15-20 minutes

1	**cup pollock fillets, cooked**
1/2	**cup onion, minced**
2	**T. butter**
1/3	**cup bread crumbs**
1	**egg, beaten**
1	**tsp. dried dill**
2	**T. fresh parsley**

Saute onion in butter; remove from heat and add remaining ingredients, mixing well. Form into 4 patties and return patties to pan, adding more butter if needed. Fry until golden brown. Garnish with lemon wedges and fresh parsley sprigs.

Creamed Pompano

Serves: 3-4
Prep Time: 15-25 minutes

1   lb. pompano fillets
2/3 can condensed cream of mushroom soup
2   T. milk
      dash cayenne pepper
      parsley sprigs

Place fillets in oblong baking dish. Stir in soup, milk and pepper; spoon over fish. Cover with vented plastic wrap and microwave on high for 6-8 minutes or until fish centers begin to flake. Let stand for 1-2 minutes before serving.

Whole Baked Pompano

Serves: 4
Prep Time: 30-35 minutes

2-3 lbs. pompano   **2   T. capers**
2   T. butter   **1   tsp. parsley, chopped**
1/8 tsp. paprika   **1   tsp. chives, chopped**
1/8 tsp. nutmeg   **2   tsp. lemon juice**
2   T. white wine   **1/2 tsp. salt**
3   T. butter

Combine 2 T. butter, paprika and nutmeg and rub over pompano. In baking dish, pour wine over fish, cover and bake for 20-25 minutes at 350 degrees. Melt 3 T. butter and add remaining ingredients to form sauce. Transfer fish to serving platter and pour butter sauce over fish.

Fish In A Skillet

Serves: 4
Prep Time: 20-25 minutes

1-1¹/₂ lbs. pompano fillets
  6   small new potatoes, scrubbed
¹/₃   cup butter
  1   medium zucchini, sliced
  1   small yellow squash, sliced
¹/₂   tsp. salt
¹/₄   black pepper, freshly ground
  1   T. fresh dill, minced
  1   large tomato, peeled, seeded and chopped

Cook potatoes in boiling, salted water until tender; drain. Melt butter in large skillet. Add zucchini and squash; top with fish fillets. Arrange potatoes around edge. Sprinkle salt, pepper and dill over fillets. Cover and simmer for 10 minutes, or until fish flakes easily when tested with fork. Add tomato, cover and cook for 1 more minute.

Poached Garden Rockfish

Serves: 6
Prep Time: 1 hour, 20-25 minutes

6	**5-oz. rockfish fillets**
6	**large romaine lettuce leaves, parboiled**
1	**cup water**
1	**medium lemon, sliced**
1	**tsp. lemon-pepper seasoning**
1	**tsp. fresh chives, minced**
1/3	**cup sour cream or plain yogurt**
1/4	**cup zucchini, grated**
1/4	**cup sweet red pepper, diced**
1/3	**cup carrot, shredded**

Poaching liquid:

1/4	**cup white vinegar or dry white wine**
3/4	**cup clam juice**
1	**bay leaf**
2	**whole peppercorns**

In large saucepan, add lettuce leaves to boiling water. Cover and cook for 2-3 minutes or until leaves are soft and pliable. Remove and drain on paper towels. Place fish fillet in center of lettuce leaf and top with lemon slice. Fold each side of lettuce over fish; fold up ends. Carefully place fish bundles in saucepan, add poaching liquid ingredients, cover and bring to a boil. Reduce heat and simmer for 6-8 minutes or until fish flakes easily when tested with fork. In small bowl, combine remaining ingredients, chill and serve with fish.

Flavorful Rockfish With Grapes

Serves: 6
Prep Time: 45-50 minutes

6	rockfish fillets or steaks
1/4	cup Worcestershire sauce
3	T. white wine vinegar
3	T. honey
3	garlic cloves, minced
1	T. toasted sesame seeds
3/4	lb. green seedless grapes (in clusters)

Place fish fillets into oblong baking dish coated with cooking spray. Cover with aluminum foil and bake at 400 degrees for 10 minutes. Combine Worcestershire sauce, vinegar, honey and garlic in small bowl; mix well. Uncover fish and pour mixture over fillets; sprinkle sesame seeds on top. Bake (uncovered) for 10 minutes or until fish is tender and flakes easily when tested with fork. Arrange grapes around fish and bake for 5 more minutes. Spoon sauce over both.

Fish Lorraine

Serves: 4
Prep Time: 30-35 minutes

2	**lbs. orange roughy fillets**
1/2	**lb. fresh asparagus, cleaned and trimmed**
1/4	**cup butter or margarine**
1/2	**cup flour**
2	**chicken bouillon cubes**
1/2	**cup boiling water**
11/2	**cups milk**
1/3	**cup Parmesan cheese, grated**
1	**T. fresh chives, minced**

Roll each fillet around 3 asparagus spears. Place fillets in oblong, buttered baking dish. In small saucepan, melt butter and blend in flour. Dissolve bouillon cubes in water and gradually add to flour mixture. Stir in milk and cook constantly until thickened. Add cheese and stir until melted. Pour half of sauce over fish, cover and bake at 350 degrees for 10-12 minutes or until fish flakes easily when tested with fork. Place on serving platter, spooning sauce over fish. Garnish with minced chives and extra sauce. Serve with rice.

Micro-Easy Deep Sea Delite

Serves: 4
Prep Time: 20-30 minutes

1/2	lb. orange roughy fillets
2	tsp. butter
1/4	cup onion, chopped
1/4	cup celery, chopped
3/4	cup apple, unpeeled and chopped
2 1/2	cups soft bread crumbs
	dash nutmeg
	dash salt
1/4	cup walnuts, chopped (optional)
1/3	cup apple juice

In glass dish, melt butter; add onion and celery. Cover dish and microwave on high for 2 minutes. In large bowl, combine apple, bread crumbs, nutmeg, salt and walnuts. Pour apple juice and celery-onion combination over mixture and stir to moisten. In buttered baking dish, arrange fillets and spread stuffing mix over fillets. Cover with plastic wrap and microwave on high for 6-8 minutes, turning once, or until fish flakes easily when tested with fork. Let stand for 2 minutes. Garnish with additional apple slices dipped in lemon juice, if desired.

Neptune's Favorite

Serves: 4
Prep Time: 30-40 minutes

1¹/₂   lbs. orange roughy fillets
¹/₄   tsp. salt
¹/₃   cup green pepper, chopped
¹/₄   cup onion, chopped
³/₄   cup white wine
³/₄   cup cheddar cheese, shredded
¹/₃   cup seasoned bread crumbs

Season fillets with salt and place in buttered baking pan. Top fillets with green pepper and onion. Pour wine over fillets and bake at 375 degrees for 18 minutes or until fish flakes easily when tested with fork; drain. Sprinkle cheese and bread crumbs over fillets; broil 3 inches from heat for 2 minutes or until cheese melts and bread crumbs are lightly browned.

Lemon-Rice Stuffed Salmon

Serves: several
Prep Time: 1 hour, 15 minutes

1	**salmon (whole), dressed**
3/4	**cup butter**
1	**cup celery, sliced**
1	**small onion, chopped**
1	**4-oz. can mushrooms, sliced**
1/4	**tsp. thyme**
1 1/2	**tsp. salt**
1/8	**tsp. pepper**
2	**tsp. lemon peel, grated**
1/4	**cup lemon juice**
1 1/3	**cups water**
1 3/4	**cups instant rice**
4	**bacon slices**

Heat butter in frying pan, adding celery, onion and mushrooms.
Saute for 5 minutes; add thyme, salt, pepper, lemon peel and
lemon juice. Pour in water and bring mixture to a boil. Mix in
rice and cover. Remove from heat and let stand for 5 minutes.
Place stuffing in cavity of salmon and sew opening closed with
heavy thread. Place fish in greased casserole. Arrange bacon
slices over top of fish. Bake (uncovered) at 350 degrees for 1
hour or until fish flakes. Baste several times with drippings or
melted butter. Remove thread before serving.

Jack Smart
Clam Gulch, Alaska

Salmon With Hollandaise Sauce

Serves: 2-3
Prep Time: 30 minutes

2-4   salmon fillets
1   lemon, sliced
1   T. butter
3/4   cup almonds, sliced
1   pkg. Hollandaise sauce mix

Place lemon slices on top of fillets and broil. While fish is broiling, put butter in saucepan and toast almonds. Prepare Hollandaise mix according to package directions. When fillets are done, pour Hollandaise sauce over fish and garnish with toasted almonds.

Salmon Pate

Serves: 10 or more
Prep Time: 10 minutes

1   16-oz. can sockeye salmon
1   16-oz. pkg. cream cheese
1   tsp. liquid smoke
1   tsp. lemon-pepper seasoning
1-2   T. onion, dried or fresh
salt to taste
parsley (optional)
stuffed olives (optional)

Drain salmon and remove bones and skin. Flake apart and blend into softened cream cheese. Add liquid smoke, lemon-pepper, onion and salt; mix well. Put mixture into lightly oiled loaf pan or form into salmon mold. Refrigerate until well-chilled. Turn out onto serving plate. Garnish with parsley and olives. Serve with crackers.

Bette Montag
Omaha, Nebraska

Salmon Lemon Loaf

Serves: several
Prep Time: 1 hour

1	1-lb. can salmon (reserve 1/4 cup liquid)	1/8	tsp. Tabasco sauce
1	tsp. fresh lemon rind	1	tsp. pepper
2	T. lemon juice	2	eggs, slightly beaten
1/2	cup onion, chopped	1/4	cup green pepper, chopped
1 1/2	cups soft bread crumbs		

Combine flaked salmon and remaining ingredients. Spoon mixture into oiled 1-qt. loaf pan. Bake for 35-40 minutes at 350 degrees. Garnish with lemon slices and serve.

Jack Smart
Clam Gulch, Alaska

Fried Fish

Serves: 4
Prep Time: 30-45 minutes

1-2	lbs. salmon		canola or vegetable oil
	dry pancake mix	1	large onion, quartered
	bread crumbs, dried		
1	tsp. garlic powder		
1	tsp. pepper		

Cut fish into nugget- or finger-sized strips. Prepare pancake mix according to directions on package. Mix dry bread crumbs with garlic powder and pepper. Dip fish pieces first into pancake batter and then into bread crumbs. Heat oil in deep-fat fryer. Carefully place fish into hot oil. Add onion and fry until slightly dark. Remove fish and drain on paper towels. Salt fish to taste while draining.

Al Wirwas
Chatsworth, California

Poached Salmon With Watercress Sauce

Serves: 4-6
Prep Time: 1 hour, 20-30 minutes

4-6	**salmon steaks, 3/4 inch thick**
3	**green onions, chopped**
3/4	**cup dry white wine**
1/4	**cup tarragon vinegar**
1/3	**cup bottle clam juice**
1	**cup plain yogurt**
1	**T. fresh lime juice**
1	**T. lime zest**
1/4	**cup fresh watercress, minced**
1	**T. Dijon mustard**
1/2	**tsp. sugar**

In large skillet, arrange salmon steaks with onions in single layer. Add wine, vinegar and clam juice; bring to a boil over medium heat. Cover and gently poach salmon for 10 minutes or until flaky when tested with fork. Transfer to serving platter and cover. Boil poaching liquid down to 1/4 cup. Cool completely; add yogurt, lime juice and zest, sugar, watercress, mustard and sugar. Blend well with whisk. Pour sauce over fish. Garnish with additional watercress sprigs and lime slices. Cover and chill for 1 hour. Serve.

Stuffed Salmon

Serves: 8
Prep Time: 1 hour

1	**3-lb. salmon, dressed**
2	**T. butter**
3/4	**cup mushrooms, sliced**
1	**small carrot, diced**
1/8	**tsp. thyme**
1/8	**tsp. basil**
3/4	**cup water**
2	**T. lemon peel, grated**
1	**cup instant rice**
1/2	**cup green onion, chopped**

Melt butter in skillet and add mushrooms and carrot, sauteeing for 5 minutes. Add thyme, basil, water and lemon peel. Bring to a boil and add rice and green onion. Cover and remove from heat; let stand for 5 minutes. Rinse salmon, pat dry and fill cavity with rice stuffing. Wrap fish in aluminum foil, place in shallow baking pan and bake at 400 degrees for 30-40 minutes or until fish is flaky and tender.

Elegant Salmon Mousse

Serves: 6-8
Prep Time: 8-9 hours

2	7³/₄-oz. cans sockeye red salmon or
1	lb. cooked fresh salmon
2	T. plain gelatin (2 envelopes)
²/₃	cup bottled clam juice
2	T. capers
2	scallions, chopped
¹/₂	cup lemon juice
1	T. fresh dill
8	drops Tabasco
1	pt. heavy whipping cream, chilled
	salad oil
³/₄	cup sour cream
	dash salt
1	tsp. lemon juice
	watercress or parsley sprigs

Sprinkle gelatin over cold clam juice in saucepan. When softened, stir gelatin over very low heat until completely dissolved. Set aside to cool (at room temperature). In blender or food processor, puree salmon, capers, scallions, lemon juice, dill, Tabasco and gelatin-clam syrup. Whip cream in chilled bowl with chilled beaters until stiff. Fold salmon puree into whipped cream. Continue to fold gently until mixture is even in color. Coat salmon well with salad oil and fill with mousse mixture. Refrigerate for 6-8 hours or overnight. Unmold carefully. To "ice" mousse, combine sour cream, salt and lemon juice. Spread "icing" carefully over entire mousse. Garnish with watercress or parsley sprigs. Serve well-chilled.

Herbed Salmon Terrine With Aspic

Serves: 6-8
Prep Time: 5 hours, 30 minutes

1	lb. smoked salmon
3	day-old bread slices (white), crusts removed
2	egg whites
1¼	cups heavy cream
¼	tsp. salt
	dash grd. black pepper
¼	tsp. ginger
¼	tsp. allspice
1½	T. lemon peel, grated
1	tsp. fresh lemon juice
1	cup shredded carrots
2	T. parsley

2	T. dill
2	T. tarragon
2	T. chives
2	T. basil (thyme or majoram)
2	cups rice, cooked

Aspic:

1	pkg. unflavored gelatin
¼	cup cold water
½	cup dry white wine
2	T. dry sherry
	dash salt and pepper

Chop salmon into small pieces; dice bread and add to fish. Beat 1 egg white until light and fluffy. Add ¼ cup cream, salt, pepper, ginger, allspice, ½ T. lemon peel and juice. Whisk to blend. Pour mixture over fish and bread; chill for 2 hours; mix in blender or food processor and puree in small amounts while adding carrots. Chill 1 hour. In chilled bowl, beat remaining egg white until stiff peaks form. Slowly add remaining cream. Place fish puree bowl in larger bowl of ice. (Keep mixture well-chilled.) Fold cream and egg whites gently into puree. Divide mixture in half, add herbs to one half. Butter 1-qt. terrine mold or glass loaf pan. Place 1 cup cooked rice on bottom of pan and press lightly. Pour fish puree with herbs on top of rice. Add second layer of rice and pour remaining fish puree over top. Smooth surface. Bake 1 hour at 325 degrees in preheated oven until firm. Cool slowly in water bath; refrigerate.

To prepare aspic, dissolve gelatin in cold water. Briefly heat wine and sherry; add salt and pepper, gelatin, stirring to blend. Cool. Decorate top with whole sprigs of herbs, carefully pour aspic over salmon loaf. Refrigerate.

Easy Court Bouillon

Serves: several
Prep Time: 1 hour

8-10	**lbs. salmon (whole)**	**1**	**medium carrot, sliced**
1	**cup dry white wine or champagne**	**1**	**celery stalk and leaves**
2	**cups water**	**1**	**bay leaf**
1	**medium onion, sliced**	**1/2**	**tsp. dried thyme**
6	**whole peppercorns**	**1/8**	**tsp. salt**

Combine all ingredients, adding more water (if needed) to cover fish. Place in large saucepan to poach or cut fish in sections and poach one section at a time.

Chris' Lemon Salmon

Serves: 4
Prep Time: 20 minutes

4	**salmon fillets**	**4-8**	**T. olive oil or Italian salad dressing**
2	**lemons, sliced**		**salt and pepper**
	parsley		

On sheet of aluminum foil, slice 1 lemon into 1/4-inch slices. Lay salmon fillets on top of lemon slices. Pour oil or dressing onto salmon. Season fillets with salt and pepper. Slice and arrange a second row of lemons on top of fillets. Wrap foil around salmon and seal edges. Place on hot grill for 8-10 minutes per side. (Oil and lemon will keep salmon moist and seasoned.) Serve over rice pilaf or wild rice. Garnish with lemon wedges and parsley. Cajun spices or onions can be substituted for more zesty flavor!

R. Christopher Mathis
York, Pennsylvania

Grilled Shark With Ginger Glaze

Serves: 4
Prep Time: 30-40 minutes

2   lbs. shark steaks
2   T. cooking oil
2   T. Russian dressing

Glaze:
1/3   cup Russian salad
      dressing
1/2   c. frozen concentrate

orange juice, thawed
1/4   cup brown sugar,
      packed
2   tsp. ginger
1 1/2   tsp. dried or fresh
      orange peel
1   tsp. celery seed
      fresh mint leaves

Combine oil and salad dressing; brush steaks generously with mixture. Grill steaks over hot coals 6 inches from heat, turning once. Fish is done when flaky. To prepare glaze, combine all glaze ingredients (except mint leaves) in small saucepan. Cook over low heat for 5-6 minutes, stirring constantly. Pour some over steaks and garnish with fresh mint leaves.

Summer Treat

Serves: 4-6
Prep Time: 25-30 minutes

1   lb. shark steaks, cut
    into bite-sized pieces
6   small yellow or
    zucchini squash
3   T. oil
2   garlic cloves, minced
1/2   cup onion, chopped
    salt and pepper to taste

1   T. fresh hot pepper,
    chopped
2   cups fresh tomatoes,
    peeled, seeded, and
    chopped
2   tsp. fresh marjoram,
    minced

Wash and slice squash into thin slices. (Do not peel.) In large skillet, heat oil and briefly saute garlic and onion. Add squash and saute for 2-3 minutes. Mix in pepper, tomatoes, marjoram and shark pieces. Season with salt and pepper. Simmer for 8-10 minutes or until shark is tender and flakes easily.

Deep-Fried Smelt

Serves: 4-6
Prep Time: 15 minutes

2	**lbs. smelt**	**1**	**cup dry bread crumbs**
2	**eggs, beaten**		**cooking oil**

Alternate dipping smelt in beaten egg and bread crumbs to coat thoroughly. Heat oil to 370 degrees; fry smelt for 3 minutes or until brown and tender. Drain. Serve with dipping sauce.

Curried Mayonnaise Dipping Sauce

Serves: several
Prep Time: 1 hours, 15 minutes

1	**cup mayonnaise**	**1/2**	**tsp. parsley**
1/4	**cup milk**	**1**	**T. pimiento**
1	**tsp. curry powder**		

Combine mayonnaise, milk, curry powder, parsley and pimiento; mix thoroughly. Chill for 1 hour. Serve with fried smelt.

Smelt Into Sardines

Serves: several (yields 1 pint)
Prep Time: 1 hour, 20 minutes

1	**pt. smelt, cleaned**	**3**	**T. vinegar**
2	**T. cooking oil**	**1**	**T. salt**

Combine all ingredients in pressure cooker. Cook at 10 lbs. pressure for 1 hour, 20 minutes.

Daniel Tatomer
Romulus, Michigan

Smelt Roma

Serves: 4-6
Prep Time: 1 hour

2-3	lbs. smelt, dressed	1/4	cup fresh parsley, finely chopped
2	garlic cloves, minced		
1-1¹/₂	onions, sliced	2	T. fresh oregano, minced
1/4	cup olive oil		
1	28-oz. can whole Italian tomatoes	1/2	tsp. each salt
		1/2	tsp. pepper
1	6-oz. can tomato paste	2	tsp. garlic powder
1	tsp. sugar	1	cup mozzarella cheese, shredded grated
1/4	cup Parmesan cheese,		

Saute garlic and onion in oil until tender. Add remaining ingredients, except smelt and cheese; blend well. Cover and simmer for 30 minutes, stirring frequently. Spread hot sauce in oblong baking dish. Arrange smelt in single layer down center of dish on top of sauce. Sprinkle mozzarella and Parmesan cheese over smelt and bake at 400 degrees for 15-20 minutes or until fish is tender and flaky.

Tomato Basil Dipping Sauce

Serves: several
Prep Time: 20-30 minutes

2	lbs. fried smelt	2	large tomatoes, peeled, seeded and diced
1	garlic clove, minced		
1	T. onion, minced		
1	tsp. oil	2/3	cup fresh basil, chopped

Saute garlic and onion in oil for 2 minutes, stirring constantly until onion is translucent. Add tomatoes and simmer (uncovered) on low heat for approximately 15 minutes, stirring frequently. Add basil and simmer for 1 more minute.

Tex-Mex Steamed Snapper

Serves: 4
Prep Time: 40-50 minutes

2 whole red snappers, cleaned and boned with heads and tails intact
1/4 cup chopped black olives
1 4-oz. can green chilis
5 green onions, chopped
2 T. dry white wine
2 tsp. chili powder
1/4 tsp. salt
1 T. fresh coriander, minced

Rinse fish in cold water and pat dry. On cutting board, cut 3-4 1/4-inch incisions in each side of fish. Set aside. Combine olives, chilis and onions. Place half of mixture in single layer on ceramic platter large enough to hold both fish. Place fish on olive mixture and cover with remaining olive mixture. Sprinkle wine, chili powder, salt and coriander over fish. Transfer platter to steamer rack of fish poacher and place over boiling water. Cover and steam for 15 minutes or until fish flakes easily when tested with fork. Remove platter from steamer and spoon hot sauce (recipe follows) over fish.

Snapper Hot Sauce

Serves: several
Prep Time: 10 minutes

1/3 cup chicken broth
1/4 cup dry white wine
3 T. hot sauce
2 garlic cloves, minced
2 tsp. chili powder
1/2 tsp. ground ginger

In small saucepan, combine all ingredients and heat for 2 minutes. Serve as dip with red snapper.

Double Ocean Delite

Serves: 8
Prep Time: 30-40 minutes

2	lbs. snapper fillets
2	T. butter
1/4	tsp. lemon-pepper seasoning
1/2	cup onion, chopped
1/2	tsp. dried parsley
1	16-oz. can tomatoes, undrained
3 1/2	oz. crabmeat
1/2	cup mozzarella cheese, shredded

In baking pan, melt butter; add snapper fillets and sprinkle lemon-pepper over top. Mix in onion, parsley and tomatoes; flake crabmeat over fish. Bake at 400 degrees or until fish is flaky and tender. Remove and sprinkle cheese on fish. Return to oven until cheese melts.

Stuffed Sole Florentine

Serves: 6
Prep Time: 45-55 minutes

1¹/₂	lbs. sole fillets	¹/₄	tsp. pepper
2	T. butter	2	T. flour
¹/₃	cup onion, chopped	1¹/₄	cups milk
1	small jar marinated artichokes	³/₄	cup mozzarella cheese, grated
1	10-oz. pkg. frozen spinach	1	tsp. Worcestershire sauce
1	cup rice, cooked	¹/₂	tsp. dried mustard
¹/₂	tsp. dill		

In saucepan, melt 1 T. butter and lightly saute onion. Add artichokes and spinach, cooking for 2 minutes. Add rice, dill and pepper; remove from heat. Put half of spinach mixture on top of sole fillets. Roll up fillets, fasten with toothpicks and place in lightly greased shallow baking dish. Bake at 400 degrees for 15-20 minutes or until fish is flaky and tender. In separate saucepan, melt 1 T. butter and stir in flour. Remove from heat and gradually pour in milk. Add remaining ingredients and cook over moderate heat, stirring frequently. Pour over stuffed fish.

Northwest Petrale Sole

Serves: 4
Prep Time: 30 minutes

2	lbs. petrale sole	1	10-oz. can cream of shrimp soup
1	lb. pink shrimp parsley to taste		thyme to taste

Form fillets into ovenproof soup bowls. Add shrimp and cover with soup. Sprinkle parsley and thyme on top. Bake in preheated oven 20 minutes at 350 degrees. Serve with rice.

Bruce Bouvia
Astoria, Oregon

Sole Supreme With Avocado Sauce

Serves: 4-6
Prep Time: 20-30 minutes

- **2 lbs. sole fillets**
- **2 ripe avocados**
- **4 T. fresh lime juice**
- **1 tsp. salt**
- **2 garlic cloves, crushed**
- **2 T. mayonnaise**
- **2 T. sour cream**
- **3 dashes hot pepper sauce**
- **1 cup flour**
- **1 tsp. salt**
- **2 tsp. freshly ground black pepper**
- **3 T. cooking oil**
- **2 limes, sliced**

Halve avocado lengthwise, removing pit. With spoon, scrape avocado from skin and put in blender or food processor. Add lime juice, salt, garlic, mayonnaise, sour cream and hot pepper sauce. Blend until smooth. Cover tightly and chill sauce until serving time. Combine flour, salt and black pepper on plate; mix. Dredge fillets in seasoned flour, shaking off excess. In large skillet, heat oil over medium-high heat until almost smoking. Add fillets and cook for approximately 3 minutes on each side or until golden brown. Serve with avocado sauce and garnish with remaining lime slices.

Meals Of The Rockies

Rocky Mountain Highs

Anglers who think of the Rocky Mountains think trout. In most cases, this means cutthroats and rainbows; although, to the far north, steelhead and salmon run well up into the Continental Divide on the Salmon, Snake and Clearwater Rivers. Oddly enough, trout received little attention in early years. Indians, flushed with the Spanish gift of horses, opted for elk, deer, sheep and bison. Only the Nez Perce, the tribe that helped Lewis and Clark cross the backbone of North America, used fish as a diet staple.

Mountain men, explorers and, to a great extent, the early naturalists were so busy burning beavers into fodder for hats, filling in blank spaces on maps and sketching game animals and birds, that fish got even less attention than rattlesnakes! Naturalists like Prince Maximilian, who brought along the splendid Swiss artist, Karl Bodmer, and hired

Sacajawea's husband, Toussaint Charbonneau, as an inter-
preter, concentrated more on "the wildlife, the Indians and
the look of the land itself" than fish.

Naturalists Nuttall and Townsen named birds—Nuttall's
woodpecker and Townsen's warbler. Catlin painted
Indians. A few may have measured fish, but the naturalists
seemed more interested in the obvious.

Townsen discovered at the Green River Trappers rendezvous of 1833 that "the fish in a small stream averaged
about 15 to 16 inches in length." These were cutthroat trout,
no doubt.

Natives And Emigrants

As population moved west, brook trout followed on steam
and pack trains. Today, most alpine lakes have brook trout.
German browns, which were common in Michigan waters,
joined the mix. Some of the best fishing in Montana is for
Clark Fork browns.

A few optimists stocked bigger lakes, like Idaho's Coeur
d'Alene with landlocked salmon and their delicious little
cousin, kokanee. Golden trout larger than those in their
natal Sierras now swim in Wyoming Lakes.

Others spread lake trout, which were taken from Great
Lakes spawning streams as fry, into likely (and unlikely)
waters. Most of the big lakes in the West have lakers. Some
of the best waters include Flathead Lake in Montana and
Idaho's Priest Lake. Freshwater shrimp, if the right type,
are also common. They are used to feed the kokanee,
which share laker temperature preferences, and provide
bite-sized chunks of protein for lakers or mackinaw in the
western United States, togue in Maine and gray trout in
Canada.

To the south of the Continental Divide, settlers quickly

introduced bass and panfish. New species eventually joined the mix in reservoirs. Big Colorado impoundments now offer striped and black bass. Such reservoirs also act as settling basins to clean river flows, improving trout fishing but threatening native species of chubs and other muddy water fish.

Cutthroats Considered

Given the rather lurid history of the Mountain range, it's appropriate that the most common trout is the cutthroat—named for its red blushing cheeks. Cuts don't jump like tarpon, fight like steelhead or look as pretty as goldens, but they do fin some of the most spectacular and beautiful waters of the West. Even better, they seem more than willing to hit flies, lures and bait. As a result, when in competition with browns or rainbows for habitat they usually lose.

Yellowstone Park, the Snake River and most Idaho streams offer quality cutthroat action. As you move south you get Paiute, Greenback, Bonneville, Colorado and Lahontan cutthroats. All of these are fun to catch, release or eat.

While rainbows and cutthroat trout finned in streams, rivers and lakes, Dolly Varden (a western char) offered dandy action on Idaho and Montana waters. This beautiful fish was supposedly named after a character in Charles Dicken's *Barnaby Rudge* whose dress also sported lavender spots. These unappreciated fish are in decline and some suggest soon to reach endangered status in Continental Divide waters.

Today, fishermen can catch and admire these fish in Idaho's St. Joe, Coeur d'Alene and other waters. The biggest Dolly Vardens, locally known as "bull trout," come from the waters of Pend Oreille, an Idaho lake so clear and so deep that the U.S. Navy uses it for underwater research!

Trout fishing and mountain streams like this one go together.

Watering The West

"Understand water, and you understand the West." The Rocky Mountains' western slopes collect much more rain and snow than the steeper east. At the south end of the Continental Divide, Arizona and New Mexico are downright arid. Los Angeles has its eye on pumping Colorado River water for years. Denver takes 800 million gallons a month from Dillon Reservoir on the west slope and pumps it over the divide to the arid east via a 23-mile tunnel.

Range water wars were common in early years. When populations increased and the depression raged, dams went up. Muddy waters of the Colorado River and its tributary streams received concrete plugs by the dozen. Nifty settling basins behind dams helped improve water quality downstream. Species changed. Chub and sucker fishing were replaced by some of the best trout fishing in America.

Steep-banked Western reservoirs offer challenges unknown in a more gentle land. Wild fluctuations in water levels can mean a drop of a foot to 18 inches a day. Largemouth bass do not do well here because spawning beds can dry before fry escape. Largemouths also need stick-ups and cover; Western reservoirs have more sand bars and steep, rocky banks. Smallmouth and, in bigger reservoirs like Lake Mead, stripers do well. In the north, walleye can be found. Most of the larger reservoirs hold lake trout that feed on kokanee. They also hold the usual mix of warm-water panfish at lower latitudes and elevations; pike can be found, too.

Popularization And Population

When mountain men took advantage of the craze for beaver hats, which ran into the middle of the 19th Century, they had no idea that the waters and backwaters where they trapped would draw crowds. Most people moseyed into Colter's Hell and Yellowstone to rendezvous or be near hot water in winter. But to come to the mountains for fish? Even the English and European sportfishermen rarely fished those waters.

Trout Next Door

Thanks to the piscatorial certainty that the quality of fishing rises in direct proportion to the distance from home, it's clear that anglers' meccas like Yellowstone's Madison River remain "bring your own rock" propositions. Jet boaters on the Snake's Hells Canyon also experience crowding on holiday weekends or during the "keep" steelhead season.

Idaho's Henry's Fork, Colorado's Green or Gunnison and a library of other Continental Divide waters mob up all summer, too. Some states license guides and restrict passage with permits. Other states only limit outfitter numbers, and anyone with a raft and ambition can get into trouble on their own. Such "pistacorially urbanized" waters will become more, not less, crowded.

Fortunately, there's usually something with better, less popularized fishing just over the hill from rivers that collect as

much writer's ink as spring runoff. Rather than the Snake
River's crowded waters in Jackson Hole, savvy anglers can
try the Gros Vente River. Instead of Idaho's Henry's Fork,
wise fly flingers consider catch-and-release cutthroat in the
St. Joe River. Rather than suffer the competition of Mead
houseboaters and the distractions of bikini-clad jet skiers,
striped bass addicts can drop down to the Colorado River.

Railroad Trout And Conservation
In the 1950s, American railroad dining cars featured local
fish. With four major railroads crossing the Continental
Divide, vast numbers of rainbow trout (most were fresh
from local waters) were put aboard passenger liners. Such
commercial operations didn't do much for the fishery. As
early as the 1900s, savvy states realized there was more
money from trout caught by sport anglers than eaten by
train passengers, so they started to cut limits and decrease
legal fishing days. As a result, most of the store-bought
trout eaten in America are now raised in southern Idaho
along spring creeks.

Slots and limits or catch-and-release seem the rules on the
best waters today. In Idaho's Snake River, for example, you
can catch the massive sturgeon that lurk in deep holes but
you must release them. Salmon that make it to spawning
headwaters are protected, and wild steelhead, bull trout
and a host of others also are safeguarded.

Angler Limits
The best known fisheries, like Yellowstone Lake or the
Madison River, seem to be most affected by growing fishermen populations; even catch-and-release won't solve the
crush on smaller waters.

Quota systems limit fishing access in the same way that
Western hunters now need to draw tags to hunt popular
species. This isn't altogether a bad thing. It ensures "old
time" quality fishing.

The Best In The Mountain West

English fishermen and American fly fishermen lust to try England's Test or Avon. In America, the Madison, Yellowstone, Green and Snake offer historic connections to angling's past. Such waters seem best met with a guide who eases anglers into the very competitive fishing over savvy trout.

Flush fishermen can add the wonderful lake trout action in Canada. Great Slave Lake kicks out regular line-test laker limits. A host of Canadian waters add pike and walleyes on a drive-in or fly-in basis.

Anglers in the mountain states should, like locals, consider lesser known waters like Idaho's St. Joe, and freestone and beaver-dammed creeks with names like Deer, Bear and Squirrel offer the best moving water fishing in the West.

Lakes in the Jim Bridger and other wilderness areas add still-water action year-round. Snake and Clearwater steelhead for the frigid-finger fishermen in the winter, and splendid striper and black-bass fishing in Lake Mohave or Mead are always great opportunities, too.

New Mexico: Land Of Contrasts

Serves: 6-8

Latin cooks do wonderful things with fish. This scrumptious meal, which includes an enchilada, authentic Spanish rice, a California guacamole and a lovely tropical dessert, is out of this world. You might serve refried beans, salsa and a few hot corn or flour tortillas on the side.

Entree: Enchilada Pesca

4	cups cooked flaked fish
2	10-oz. cans enchilada sauce
2	10-oz. cans red chili sauce
2	medium onions, chopped
3	large hard-cooked eggs
2	cups cheddar cheese, grated
2	cups Monterey Jack cheese, grated
1	6-oz. can pitted black olives
1	4-oz. can green chilis, diced
12	tortillas (corn or flour)

Bring 1 can enchilada and 1 can chili sauce to a boil. Cover chopped onions with water, boil for 3 minutes and drain. Chop hard-cooked eggs, mix grated cheeses, drain olives and chilis and fish and onions; place each in separate dish. Reserve 1/2-cup cheese and a few olives for topping. Butter 9x13-inch baking dish.

Dip tortilla in warm reserved sauce (tortillas roll easier if dipped in warm sauce). Spoon 1/12 filling into tortilla and tuck its edges under in a smooth roll against the end of the pan. Repeat until side-by-side rolled tortillas fill pan; mix and pour remaining cans of enchilada and chili sauce over filling. Top with reserved cheese and olives. Bake for 40 minutes at 350 degrees. Top with sour cream and/or guacamole.

Side Dish No.1: Spanish Rice

2	T. vegetable oil
1	small onion, chopped
1	cup rice

2   cups chicken stock
1   small fresh tomato, chopped
1   tsp. dry taco seasoning
$1/8$ tsp. salt
$1/4$ tsp. pepper

Heat oil in skillet over medium heat. Add onion and fry until light brown. Add rice and cook until transparent, about 3 minutes. Add stock, tomato, taco seasoning, salt and pepper. Bring to a boil, lower heat; then cover and simmer for 20 minutes. Fluff with fork before serving. Rice should be dry. (Note: Add more taco seasoning for hotter taste.)

Side Dish No.2: Guacamole

2   large ripe avocados
2   T. lemon juice
1   small fresh tomato, chopped
2-3 T. red or green taco sauce

Cut avocados in half, remove pits and scoop out pulp with spoon. In small bowl, mash pulp with fork. Add lemon juice, tomato and taco sauce; mix well and chill. Serve with enchiladas or as a dip with Tortilla chips.

Dessert: Mango Cream

1   large orange
5   large ripe mangoes
$1/4$ cup sugar
2   cups whipping cream
3   T. powdered sugar
$3/4$ cup almonds, chopped
     Maraschino cherries

Peel orange, remove seeds and cut into $1/2$-inch-thick pieces. In blender, beat chilled mangoes until smooth. Add sugar (more sugar provides a sweeter taste) and mix. In electric mixer, add cream and beat until slightly thickened. Add powdered sugar and continue to beat until cream is whipped. Fold cream, oranges and nuts into mango mixture. Serve in parfait glasses and top with almonds and cherries.

Cornish Miner's Delights

Serves: 4-6

After gold panners and rocker-box operators skimmed the cream off gold from stream beds, the big gold companies went to hard-rock mining and deep shafts. Cornish men from South England had mined coal and other materials for nearly 1,000 years. They brought with them traditional Cornish pies that miners could take cold into the mine and heat on lanterns. Such pies also became popular in Canada. Slather on some malt vinegar, add a few vegetables and a nice desert and this meal will warm you up on a cold day. Best of all, you can make Cornish Pasties in advance and freeze them until needed.

Soup: Carrot Soup

4	T. butter
2	cups yellow onions, finely diced
10	large carrots, peeled and chopped
5	cups chicken stock

Melt butter in saucepan and add onions. Cover and cook for 30 minutes over low heat. Add carrots and stock. Bring to a near boil, reduce heat and cook for 30 more minutes. Blend soup in blender until smooth. (This is easier if done a little at a time and transferred into new pot.) Season soup as desired and serve. (Note: A tablespoon of sour cream and a sprinkling of dill offer a nice Russian flavor.)

Entree: Canadian/Cornish Fish Pasties

4$^1/_2$	cups flour	$^1/_3$	cup sherry
1	tsp. salt	1	tsp. thyme
1	tsp. curry powder	$^1/_4$	tsp. salt
$^1/_2$	tsp. paprika	$^1/_4$	tsp. pepper
24	T. shortening	1	tsp. sugar
4	cups cooked fish, cut into $^3/_4$-inch cubes	2	T. flour
		2	medium tart apples, sliced
2	cups potatoes, cubed		
1	cup carrots, sliced	1	egg white
1	onion, coarsely chopped	1	T. water

Combine flour with salt, curry powder and paprika. Cut in shortening until flour is well-blended and pieces are pea-size. Mix 1 T. water into flour mixture at a time until dough forms a ball as it's stirred. Wrap ball in waxed paper and chill. Mix potatoes with fish, carrots, onion, sherry and seasonings. Mix sugar with flour and apples.

Heat oven to 350 degrees. Lightly grease cookie sheet. Mix egg white with water. Divide dough into 24 balls. Roll two balls out on floured surface into circles about 1/4 inch thick. Place 3/4 cup of fish filling into center of 1 dough circle, leaving 1-inch margin free. Top with a few apple slices. Brush margin with egg mixture. Cover with second dough circle. Use a fork to crimp circles and flute edges. Brush top with egg wash and bake for 1 hour.

Side Dish: Sliced Zucchini

4	small zucchini, sliced diagonally
	salt and pepper to taste
1/4	tsp. sesame oil (optional)

Steam zucchini in steamer or colander over boiling water until cooked yet crisp. Add salt and pepper to taste and, for a nice nutty flavor, sprinkle sesame oil over zucchini.

Dessert: Chocolate Fudge Cheese Cake

Crust:

1 1/3	cups flour		1/2	cup firm butter
1/4	cup sugar		1	egg yolk
1	T. lemon peel			

Filling:

12	oz. cream cheese		3/4	cup sugar
2	eggs		1	tsp. lemon juice

Chocolate Fudge Sauce:

1	oz. unsweetened chocolate		2	T. butter
			3	T. hot water
8	T. sugar		1	T. corn syrup
1	tsp. amaretto			

Sour Cream Topping:

3¹/₂ tsp. sugar
  1 cup sour cream

2 T. amaretto or your
   favorite liquor

Preheat oven to 350 degrees. Mix flour, sugar and lemon peel together. Cut in butter with pastry blender or knife until mixture resembles coarse meal. Blend in egg yolk with whisk or fork. Then work dough into ball with your hands. Press dough into 9-inch pie plate. Fill crust with dry, uncooked beans to keep crust from puffing while cooking. Bake for 20 minutes and remove from oven.

Combine filling ingredients and mix well. Pour into warm pie shell and bake at 350 degrees for 40 minutes or until set (test with toothpick). Remove from oven.

Combine topping ingredients in bowl. Pour topping over filling and bake for 10 more minutes. Remove from oven and cool.

To make chocolate fudge sauce, melt chocolate and butter slowly over low heat in heavy saucepan. Stir in hot water. Add sugar and corn syrup and stir until smooth. Bring to a boil and hold for 9 minutes over lowest possible heat, stirring constantly. Remove from heat and cool for 10 minutes. Stir in amaretto and cool to room temperature. Spread sauce in 1-inch-wide strip in middle of cheese cake. Use knife blade to pull sauce to edge of pie for decoration. Refrigerate until serving.

Fast Fixin' Mountain Meal

Serves: 4-6

This is an easy way to fix 6- to 12-inch trout at home or out camping. If you camp, you can prepare the dry ingredients in advance. Put them in a large plastic bag and toss the trout into the bag to coat. The nuts and/or Parmesan cheese adds a different flavor to the fish then just grilled or fried trout. Asparagus keeps well in camp, and, even after you run out of usual bread, you can enjoy Irish Soda Bread, a favorite of the many Irish that filled the soldiers' ranks in the early West. Toast the leftover bread for breakfast.

Entree: Nutty-Fried Trout

4   **medium trout (or kokanee salmon)**
1/2   **cup flour**
1/4   **tsp. garlic powder**
1/4   **cup walnuts, finely chopped**
1/8   **tsp. salt**
1/8   **tsp. pepper**
2   **eggs, beaten**
1/4   **cup cooking oil or butter**

Clean trout and pat dry. Combine flour, garlic powder, walnuts, salt and pepper in shallow dish. Dip trout into beaten eggs, then into flour/walnut mixture. Set trout aside on waxed paper or dish for 10 minutes (this will help set the crust on the trout). Heat oil or melt butter in skillet over medium heat. Fry trout until brown, about 7 minutes per side or until trout flakes with fork. (Variation: Add almonds or Parmesan cheese to flour mixture in place of walnut.)

Side Dish No.1: Asparagus With Basil Vinaigrette Dressing

1   **lb. asparagus**

Dressing:
3   **T. olive oil**
1/4   **cup red wine vinegar**
1/4   **tsp. salt**
1/2   **tsp. freshly ground pepper**
1   **T. basil leaves, chopped**
1/2   **tsp. sugar**

Rinse and remove outer skin of asparagus spears' fat-ends with potato peeler, allowing you to eat entire spears. Cook asparagus in boiling, salted water until tender, about 10-15 minutes. Drain and immediately rinse under cold water to stop cooking and set the most attractive bright green color. Refrigerate and serve cold topped with vinaigrette dressing.

Combine all dressing ingredients in jar; shake well. Prepare 1 hour before serving. Refrigerate until needed.

Side Dish No.2: Irish Soda Bread

3¹/₄	cups flour	1¹/₂	cups buttermilk
¹/₄	cup sugar	1	tsp. baking soda
2	tsp. caraway seed (optional)	1	cup candied citron (optional)
1¹/₂	tsp. baking powder	1	egg
1	tsp. salt	1	T. water

Preheat oven to 375 degrees. Butter cookie sheet and combine flour, sugar, caraway seed, baking powder and salt in large bowl. Mix buttermilk and baking soda together and gradually add to flour mixture, stirring with spoon until blended. Add citron and mix dough into smooth, round loaf.

Beat egg and water together and brush loaf with egg mixture. Place large round loaf on cookie sheet and bake for about 1 hour or until bread browns. Remove from oven and cool on rack. (Note: You can cook this in a Dutch oven covered with campfire coals.)

Dessert: Chunky Apple Walnut Cake

3	cups pippin apples, coarsely chopped
1	cup sugar
1	tsp. baking soda
1	tsp. cinnamon
1	cup flour
¹/₄	tsp. salt
2	T. Calvados or Applejack
1	egg
¹/₄	cup vegetable oil
1	cup walnuts, chopped

Lemon Sauce (optional):

¹/₄	cup sugar
3	T. flour
1	cup water
3	T. lemon juice
1	T. butter

Combine apples with sugar, baking soda, cinnamon, flour and

salt immediately after peeling to avoid discoloration. Add Calvados, egg, oil and walnuts. Mix and pour into greased and ·floured 9x9-inch pan. Bake for 45 minutes at 350 degrees. Do not over-bake or it will get dry. Serve hot or cold with whipped cream or lemon sauce.

For lemon sauce, combine sugar and flour in saucepan. Add water and lemon juice. Cook until thickened over medium heat. Add butter and stir until melted. Serve over Apple cake.

Totally Trout
Serves: 4-6

Trophy trout deserve a peerless presentation—even when summer heat limits menu choices to warm entrees and cool side dishes. Big trout provide a fine focus for a formal meal. Cold soup (discovered by the British in India) sounds a bit strange, but it's a cool treat on a hot day! This classic cream soup suits both the camp cook and the home chef in search of a lunch entree or an appetizer before a large meal.

Soup: Malabar Curried Trout Soup

2	lbs. trout fillets, cut into 1-inch cubes
4	T. butter
2	cups onions, chopped
2	celery stalks, sliced
2	carrots, chopped
1	T. curry powder
4	cups fish stock or chicken broth
1	T. parsley flakes
1/3	cup uncooked rice
1	cup heavy cream or half-and-half
	salt and pepper to taste

Melt butter in saucepan and add onions, celery, carrots and curry. Cover and cook for 10 minutes over low heat or until vegetables are tender. Add stock, parsley, trout and rice. Cover and cook for 20 minutes or until fish flakes when tested with fork, and rice is tender. Add cream and simmer for 10 more minutes. Season with salt and pepper. If cooled and blended, this soup slides smoothly down the throat on hot, humid summer days. (Note: Camp cooks substitute reconstituted powdered milk for fresh.)

Salad: Mandarin Orange And Almond Salad

1	bunch fresh spinach, cleaned and trimmed
1	6^1/$_2$-oz. can mandarin oranges, drained
1	small red onion, sliced
^{3}/$_4$	cup raw mushrooms, sliced
^{1}/$_2$	cup roasted sliced almonds
^{1}/$_4$	cup roasted sesame seeds

Dressing:

6	T. olive oil
3	T. red wine vinegar
1	T. onion juice
1	T. water
	salt and pepper to taste

One hour prior to serving, remove stems and tear spinach leaves into bite-sized pieces and place in serving bowl with onions, mushrooms, almonds and sesame seeds; refrigerate. Combine dressing ingredients and pour over spinach. Toss and serve.

You might end such a classic meal over fresh fruit and nuts. Bright navel oranges, golden pears and crisp green apples peeled at the table as nutcrackers and picks pop and pry at almonds, walnuts, Hazelnuts and Brazil nuts punctuate good conversation and the last of the dinner wine.

Entree: Papa's Trout

1	4-lb. trout or steelhead	1	tsp. parsley flakes
1	stick butter	2	cups cooked rice
1	medium onion, chopped	1	6-oz. can green olives
3	celery stalks, chopped		with pimientos
1	tsp. ground sage		salt and pepper
1	tsp. thyme leaves		

Clean whole fish, pat dry and place on greased baking dish or sheet. Spread fins and tail and protect them against burning with folded aluminum foil; remove foil just before serving. (Note: if you leave the head on, replace the eye with an olive just before serving.)

Melt butter in skillet over medium heat and saute chopped onion and celery until tender. Add sage, thyme, parsley, cooked rice and drained green olives with pimentos; mix well. Stuff trout with rice just before baking. Place extra rice in buttered casserole, wait for 15 minutes then bake it with trout. (Note: Baste with any juice from trout.) Season trout with salt and pepper and bake at 350 degrees for 45 minutes or until fish flakes with fork. (Rice stuffing can be made a day early and refrigerated.)

If you like crisp, brown trout skin, baste fish with melted butter as it bakes. If you dislike skin, neatly remove it from upper side of trout before serving. Decorate trout with "scales" made from a second can of sliced green olives and a gill formed with diced red pimentos; brush with melted butter.

For a cool and spectacular summer-buffet variation, let fish cool after it cooks. Then remove skin and coat fish with seasoned mayonnaise or aspic made from fish stock. Decorate fish with sliced olive or sliced cucumber scales, black-olive fins and a pimento-stuffed olive eye. Present on a sea of chopped aspic or finely sliced lettuce.

Panfish Pleasures
Serves: 2-4

The Rocky Mountains mean trout to most who fish. However, you can find some of the best yellow perch, crappie and bluegill fishing in America in such "trout" spots as Idaho's Coeur d'Alene Lake and its tributary rivers. Even the Snake River, which is famous for steelhead, offers 100 crappie days behind its dam each spring. Best of all, you can catch your fill, because, unlike most other species, panfish thrive under fishing pressure. A bluegill appetizer, a "Krispie Crappie" entree and a perch salad suit days when coolers fill with panfish. The pineapple dessert included with this meal is easy to make. Children seem to enjoy eating the menu items in this meal, and they can easily make most of these dishes with a little help.

Appetizer: Bluegill Oriental

       2   **lbs. bluegills or other panfish fillets**
     1/2   **cup flour**
     1/2   **cup cornstarch**
       1   **tsp. salt**
    1 1/2 **tsp. baking powder**
       1   **egg**
     2/3   **cup water**
           cooking oil
           catsup
           Chinese hot mustard

Rinse and cut fillets into bite-sized pieces. Combine flour, cornstarch, salt and baking powder. Beat egg and water together and mix quickly with dry ingredients. Batter should be a bit lumpy. Heat 1-inch oil in skillet over medium heat. Dip fillets into batter and fry quickly on each side until brown, about 2-3 minutes. Drain on paper towels. Serve with catsup and mustard.

Salad: Plain Tomato Salad

       4   **medium tomatoes (fresh), sliced**

Dressing:
     1/2   **cup mayonnaise**
     1/4   **cup lemon juice**
       1   **tsp. dill weed**

Combine dressing ingredients and refrigerate for 30 minutes. Serve dressing over sliced tomatoes arranged on serving dish. Garnish with parsley.

Entree: Krispie Crappie

       2   **lbs. crappie or other panfish fillets**
       1   **stick butter**
       1   **tsp. garlic powder**

$^1/_4$ tsp. salt
$^1/_8$ tsp. pepper
3 cups Rice Krispies, finely crushed

Rinse fillets and pat dry. Melt butter in saucepan over low heat, stir in garlic powder, salt and pepper. Cut aluminum foil and place on cookie sheet. Dip fillets into butter mixture; then roll in Rice Krispies. Bake for 25 minutes at 375 degrees or until brown and the fish is flaky.

Dessert: Pineapple Freeze

1 cup milk
1 lb. marshmallows
2 cups drained crushed pineapple
$^1/_2$ pt. heavy cream
1 cup graham cracker crumbs

Heat milk in saucepan over low heat; add marshmallows and cook until melted. Remove from heat and cool. Add drained pineapple; mix. Whip cream to stiff peaks and fold into pineapple mixture. Sprinkle cracker crumbs into two ice cube trays; dividers should be removed. Spread pineapple mixture on top and freeze until firm, about 2-3 hours.

Basque Banquet
Serves: 4-6

When Basque sheep herders came West they brought Spanish and Basque dishes. While they ate a lot of lamb, fish remained a special treat. Scallops with wine and garlic make a dandy appetizer, as well as a good lunch entree.

Appetizer: Scallops With Wine And Garlic

$1^1/_2$ lbs. scallops
4 T. butter or margarine
2 green onions, minced
1 garlic clove, finely minced
$^1/_4$ tsp. salt (optional)

$^1/_4$ tsp. pepper
$^3/_4$ cup flour
2 T. olive oil
$^2/_3$ cup white wine
$^1/_4$ tsp. thyme leaves

Melt 2 T. butter in skillet over medium heat. Add onions and garlic and saute until soft. Cut scallops into ¼-inch-thick rounds. Season scallops with salt and pepper. Put flour and seasoned scallops in small paper bag and shake until scallops are coated. Melt remaining butter and oil over medium heat and saute scallops for 1 minute per side. Add wine and cover. Simmer for 5 minutes. Sprinkle thyme leaves over top and serve.

Entree: Basque-Style Paella

1	lb. fish fillets
1	large pinch saffron
2	cups water
1	lb. shrimp
12	littleneck clams or mussels
4	T. olive oil
1	onion, chopped
2	garlic cloves, minced
1	small green onion, chopped
1	cup long grain rice
2	tomatoes (fresh), cut into 1-inch cubes
½	cup dry white wine
1	bay leaf
1	tsp. paprika
1	tsp. dried thyme leaves

Cut fillets into 2-inch cubes. Soak saffron in 2 cups water for 20 minutes. Peel shrimp and remove veins. (Those lucky enough to have fresh gulf shrimp can simply twist the heads off.) If you use mussels scrub them under running water. Discard any clams or mussels that are open.

Heat oil in large skillet or paella pan and add fish cubes; brown lightly on all sides over medium heat. Remove with slotted spoon and reserve. Add onion, garlic and green pepper to pan; fry until soft. Add rice and cook until transparent. Add clams or mussels to center of pan so they are close to heat. Then add shrimp, fish, wine, bay leaf, paprika, thyme and saffron with water. Bring to a boil, lower heat and cook (uncovered) for 20 minutes or until liquid is absorbed and all ingredients are cooked. Serve with French bread.

Dessert: Burnt Cream

4   egg yolks
1   cup heavy cream
¹/₂   cup sugar
1   tsp. vanilla extract
**   sugar**

Beat egg yolks, cream, sugar and vanilla until well blended. Pour into ¹/₂-cup custard serving dishes and place in baking pan with 1¹/₂-2-inch rim. Pour water around custard dishes to within ¹/₂ inch of rim. Bake at 325 degrees for 1 hour or until done. Custard should be firm. Remove custard dishes and cool; refrigerate for 2 hours. Remove custard dishes and sprinkle sugar until tops are covered. Place under broiler, 6-8 inches from top, and brown until sugar caramelizes (about 3 minutes). Remove and refrigerate for at least 1 hour before serving.

Recipes For:

Sturgeon

Swordfish

Tilapia

Tilefish

Trout

Tuna

Turbot

Walleye

Beer-Battered Sturgeon

Serves: 2-4
Prep Time: 30 minutes

>   **sturgeon, cut into bite-sized pieces**
>   **water**
> **2-3** **cups pancake mix**
> **2** **eggs**
> **1** **can beer**
>   **cooking oil**
>   **salt to taste**

Boil sturgeon pieces in kettle of water. Skim off fat and drain fish on paper towels. Prepare pancake mix according to package directions, using eggs. Pour in your favorite beer. Dip sturgeon pieces into batter and deep-fry in oil until golden brown. Add salt to taste.

David Gardner
Menasha, Wisconsin

Smoked Sturgeon Pita Spread

Serves: 4
Prep Time: 45 minutes

> **1** **cup smoked sturgeon, flaked**
> **1/2** **cup cucumber, chopped**
> **1/2** **cup mayonnaise**
> **1** **T. chives, chopped**
> **1** **T. parsley, chopped**
> **1** **T. alfalfa sprouts**
> **3** **T. salsa (optional)**
> **4** **pita-bread halves**

Combine all ingredients (except salsa and pita bread) and refrigerate for 30 minutes or more. Stuff mixture into pita bread pockets. Spoon 1 T. salsa of top of each pocket. Serve.

Micro-Easy Sturgeon Stuffed Manicotti

Serves: 6-8
Prep Time: 1 hour

2	**cups sturgeon, flaked or cubed**
8	**manicotti shells, cooked**
1	**egg, beaten**
1	**cup cottage cheese**
3/4	**cup herb seasoned stuffing mix (dry)**
2	**T. dried parsley flakes**
1/3	**cup Parmesan cheese, grated**
	fresh parsley sprigs (optional)

Sauce:

1/4	**cup margarine**
1/4	**cup flour**
13/4	**cups milk**
1/2	**cup green onion, sliced**
1/4	**cup pimiento, chopped**
1/2	**tsp. celery salt**
1/2	**tsp. celery seed**

Prepare sauce first. In small non-metallic bowl, melt margarine. Add flour, mixing well. Whisk in milk and microwave on high for 4-6 minutes, stirring frequently. (Do not boil.) When thickened, add remaining ingredients, blending well. Pour half of sauce into oblong buttered baking dish. Set aside remaining sauce.

To prepare manicotti, boil and drain manicotti shells per package directions. In large bowl, stir egg into cottage cheese; add stuffing mix, parsley and Parmesan cheese. Blend well. Fold in sturgeon. Lightly spoon 1/2 cup mixture into each precooked manicotti shell and place in prepared sauce. Pour reserved sauce over manicotti, coating all pasta. Cover with plastic wrap, venting one corner. Microwave on medium heat for 20-25 minutes, rotating dish once or until fish flakes when tested with fork. Reglaze manicotti with pan sauce before serving. Garnish with fresh parsley sprigs, if desired.

Smoked Sturgeon Cakes

Serves: 6
Prep Time: 20-25 minutes

2	**cups smoked sturgeon, flaked**
1/2	**cup cracker crumbs**
2	**eggs, beaten**
1/2	**tsp. dried parsley flakes**
1	**tsp. dried minced onion**
1/2	**tsp. salt**
2	**T. butter**

Combine all ingredients except butter. Mix thoroughly and form mixture into cake. Saute fish cakes in butter until golden brown, turning once.

Swordfish Stir-Fry

Serves: 4
Prep Time: 20-25 minutes

1	lb. swordfish chunks
2	T. oil
2	carrots, thinly sliced
1	onion, thinly sliced
3	zucchini, thinly sliced
1/4	tsp. thyme leaves
1/4	tsp. pepper

In wok or large skillet, heat oil and add carrots, onion, zucchini and thyme. Stir-fry until slightly tender. Season swordfish with pepper and add to skillet. Stir-fry until swordfish is tender and flaky. Serve over hot bed of rice.

Seafood Kabobs

Serves: 6
Prep Time: 2-3 hours plus 30-45 minutes

1	lb. swordfish
1	lb. bay or ocean scallops
1/2	lb. bacon (cut each strip in half)
1	pt. cherry tomatoes
2	green peppers, cut into wedges
4	oz. fresh whole mushrooms
2	cups dry sherry (add more if needed)
1/4	cup soy sauce
	juice of fresh lemon
	salt and pepper to taste

Cut swordfish into 2-inch pieces. Wash and drain scallops. Thread skewer with bacon, scallop, tomato, green pepper, swordfish and mushrooms. Make sure bacon intertwines each seafood piece. Marinate in sherry and soy sauce. Chill for several hours. Add fresh lemon juice and salt and pepper. Broil under medium heat until bacon is well done. Don't overcook.

Garlic Swordfish Broil

Serves: 8
Prep Time: 20-35 minutes

> **2**   lbs. swordfish steaks
> **1**   T. butter
> **4**   garlic cloves, minced
> **1/4** tsp. pepper
> **2**   T. white wine
> **4**   T. lemon juice

In saucepan, melt butter; add garlic and saute until garlic begins to color. Season with pepper and white wine. Place swordfish steaks on broiler pan and brush with seasoned butter. Broil 4 inches from heat, basting occasionally for 10-15 minutes or until fish is tender and flaky. Sprinkle lemon juice over steaks.

Micro-Easy Herbed Swordfish Steaks

Serves: 4
Prep Time: 25-30 minutes

> **4**   swordfish steaks
> **1**   4-oz. pkg. soft cream cheese with herbs
> **1/4** cub prepared tartar sauce
> **1/2** medium cucumber, sliced into 12 circles
> **1/2** cup shredded cheddar cheese
> **1**   T. chopped fresh chives

Arrange swordfish in oblong baking dish. Combine cream cheese and tartar sauce, spreading over steaks. Cover with vented plastic wrap. Microwave on high for 7-8 minutes (rotating once) or until center of fish begins to flake when tested with fork. Top steaks with cucumber slices. Sprinkle cheddar cheese and snipped chives over steaks. Microwave (uncovered) on high for 2-3 minutes or until cheese melts. Let stand (covered) for 5 minutes.

Oven-Fried Tilapia

Serves: 4
Prep Time: 20 minutes

1	**lb. tilapia fillets**
1/8	**tsp. pepper**
2	**T. butter, melted**
1/3	**cup saltine crackers, crushed**

Season tilapia with pepper; dip in melted butter and coat with cracker crumbs. In lightly oiled, shallow baking dish, arrange fish and bake at 400 degrees for 10 minutes without turning or basting.

Tilapia Vegetable Bake

Serves: 4
Prep Time: 30-35 minutes

1	**lb. tilapia fillets, divided into 4 portions**
1	**carrot, julienned**
1/4	**lb. snow peas**
2	**medium potatoes, peeled and sliced**
1	**medium onion, sliced**
3	**T. butter, cut into pieces**
1	**tsp. basil**
	salt and pepper to taste

Place 4 tilapia portions on 4 individual sheets of aluminum foil. On each fillet, place 1/4 of carrots, snow peas, potatoes and onion. Dot with butter and sprinkle basil, salt and pepper over top. Close and seal aluminum packets and place in shallow baking dish. Bake at 400 degrees for 10-12 minutes or until fish is flaky and tender. (If cooking on grill, put foil packet over hot coals, cover grill with lid and cook for 15-20 minutes or until fish is flaky and tender when tested with fork.)

Viva L'Tilapia

Serves: 4
Prep Time: 30-40 minutes

1¹/₂-2 lbs. tilapia fillets
- **¹/₄ cup onion, chopped**
- **¹/₄ cup sweet red pepper, chopped**
- **¹/₄ cup celery, chopped**
- **3 T. butter or margarine**
- **3 T. flour**
- **salt and pepper to taste**
- **¹/₂ tsp. dried tarragon**
- **¹/₂ tsp. dried basil**
- **1¹/₄ cups milk**
- **1 cup mozzarella cheese, shredded**

In medium skillet, saute onions, sweet red pepper and celery in butter until tender. Add flour, salt and pepper, tarragon and basil; mix well. Gradually add milk and cook over medium heat, stirring constantly until thickened. Add cheese and stir until melted. Do not boil. Place fish fillets in oblong baking dish and spoon sauce evenly over fillets. Bake at 425 degrees for 8-10 minutes or until fillets flake easily when tested with fork.

Tilefish With Orange Curry Sauce

Serves: 6
Prep Time: 45-50 minutes

1¹/₂	lbs. tilefish fillets
¹/₂	cup orange yogurt
1	can mandarin oranges, drain and reserve juice
¹/₂	tsp. curry powder
2	T. oil
2	T. lime juice
¹/₄	cup almonds, toasted

Blend yogurt, 2 tsp. mandarin orange juice from can and curry powder; chill for 20 minutes. Combine oil and lime juice to baste fish. Place fish on lightly oiled rack. Grill or broil 5-6 inches from heat for 8-10 minutes or until fish is flaky and tender; turn once and baste frequently. Spoon orange curry sauce over fish. Sprinkle almonds over top and garnish with mandarin oranges.

Seasoned Bake Tilefish

Serves: 4
Prep Time: 45-50 minutes

2	lbs. tilefish, dressed
¹/₂	cup parsley, chopped
1	tsp. dried dill
¹/₄	cup green peppers, chopped
¹/₂	cup onion, chopped
2	T. lemon juice
1	medium potato, peeled and chopped
	salt and pepper to taste

Combine parsley, dill, green peppers, onion, lemon juice and potato; spread mixture inside tilefish cavity. Wrap fish in aluminum foil, sealing edges. Bake at 400 degrees for 20-30 minutes or until fish is tender. Season with salt and pepper.

Gulfshore Special

Serves: 4
Prep Time: 10-20 minutes

1-1 1/2 lbs. tilefish, cut into 1-inch steaks
1/2   tsp. salt
1/4   tsp. paprika

Salsa:
2   medium red or yellow peppers, chopped
1   medium tomato, chopped
1   medium onion, chopped
6   fresh coriander leaves, minced
1/4   tsp. ground cumin

Preheat oven broiler and oil pan. Sprinkle salt and paprika on both sides of fish; place fish on rack and broil 4 inches from heat for 5 minutes on each side. To prepare salsa, combine all ingredients in food processor or blender and process for 30 seconds. Drain before serving. Place hot fish on serving platter and spoon salsa over fish.

Baked Trout

Serves: 12
Prep Time: 12-15 hours or overnight plus 1 hour

10	lbs. whole trout
1	cup salt
3	eggs
1	pt. sauterne wine or dry vermouth
1	large onion, chopped
2	cups celery, chopped
3	lbs. bread crumbs
1/2	tsp. tarragon
1/2	tsp. garlic powder
1	tsp. sage
1/2	lb. bacon slices (thick)
8-10	bay leaves

Rub salt into fish cavities and refrigerate overnight or 12-15 hours until time to stuff fish. Rinse out remaining salt. To make stuffing, combine eggs, wine, onion, celery and bread crumbs, mixing thoroughly. Rub tarragon, garlic powder and sage into fish cavity; stuff fish. Sew up cavity or use closure rods. Cover fish with bacon slices and bay leaves. Bake at 300 degrees until probe easily penetrates fish. (Salmon can be substituted for the trout.)

John O'Toole
Alamo, Texas

Grilled Trout With Bacon And Vegetable Stuffing

Serves: 4
Prep Time: 45 minutes

4	**trout, dressed**
10	**bacon slices**
1/4	**cup onion, chopped**
1/2	**cup green pepper, chopped**
1	**small zucchini, thinly sliced**
1	**medium tomato, diced**
1/2	**cup shredded mozzarella cheese**
1	**bread slice (crumbs)**
1/2	**tsp. basil**
1/4	**tsp. garlic powder**
	lemon slices (optional)

Cut bacon into 1/2-inch pieces and cook in skillet on medium to low heat until crisp. Drain skillet and remove bacon, reserving 2 T. fat. Add onion, green pepper and zucchini to skillet; cook until tender-crisp. Stir in bacon, tomato, cheese, bread crumbs, basil and garlic powder. Rinse trout in cold water and pat dry. Stuff each cavity with vegetable mixture and tie closed with string. Place trout on lightly greased aluminum foil. Top with lemon slices, if desired. Secure foil edges to make a packet. Grill 6 inches from hot coals for 10-15 minutes per side or until fish flakes easily.

Joseph Kozlowski
Nemacolin, Pennsylvania

Breaded Sweet And Sour Fish

Serves: 4
Prep Time: 1 hour

1	lb. trout, skinned, deboned and cut into 2x3-inch pieces cornstarch	1/3	c. apple cider vinegar
		1/2	cup pineapple chunks
		1/2	carrot, shredded
		1/3	cup sweet pickles, minced
1/2	cup flour		
1	egg	1	tomato, wedge cut
1/2	cup water	1 1/2	T. cornstarch dissolved in 1/4 cup water
1/3	cup brown sugar		

Roll trout pieces in cornstarch and set aside. Combine flour, egg and water to form batter. In medium-sized pan, dissolve brown sugar and vinegar over medium heat. Add pineapple chunks, carrot, sweet pickle, tomato wedges and cornstarch. Simmer for 3-5 minutes, stirring often. Fry batter-coated pieces in hot oil for 1 minute, turn and fry for another minute. Cool, serve with sauce.

Oscar Ison
Baker City, Oregon

Trout Amandine

Serves: 2-4
Prep Time: 30-40 minutes

6	trout, cleaned cooking oil		juice from 2 lemons
		1/3	cup almonds, crushed
1/2	cup butter or margarine		

Heat cooking oil in skillet. (For enhanced flavor, grease skillet with lemon butter.) Cook fillets for 8-10 minutes over medium heat. Combine butter, lemon juice and almonds to make sauce. Brush (do not pour) sauce over fish.

A. W. Akers
Knoxville, Tennessee

Stuffed Trout With Bacon

Serves: 2
Prep Time: 1 hour, 15 minutes

1	**trout, cleaned**	**1/2**	**T. garlic powder**
6	**bacon strips**		**salt and pepper**
2	**T. onion, chopped**		**to taste**
2	**T. celery, chopped**	**1**	**egg**
1/4	**lb. butter**	**1/4**	**cup milk**
1/2	**T. thyme**	**1 1/2**	**cups bread cubes**

Fry 2 bacon strips until crisp. Saute onion and celery in butter until clear. Add spices and crumbled bacon. In small bowl, beat egg and milk together and stir in bread cubes; add to bacon mixture to make stuffing and brown. Stuff trout and wrap remaining bacon strips around trout. Bake at 325 degrees for 1 hour.

Alan Shepherd
Gettysburg, Pennsylvania

Basil-Baked Sea Trout

Serves: 4
Prep Time: 15-25 minutes

1	**lb. sea trout fillets**	**1**	**T. lemon-pepper**
2	**T. butter, melted**		**seasoning**
1/3	**cup crushed potato**	**1**	**tsp. dried basil**
	chips	**1**	**T. lemon juice**
1/3	**cup bread crumbs**		**lemon pieces (optional)**
	radish roses (optional)		

Coat trout with melted butter. Combine chips and bread crumbs, lemon-pepper and basil; dredge fish. Place fillets in lightly oiled, shallow baking dish and sprinkle lemon juice on top. Bake at 400 degrees for 10-15 minutes or until fish is flaky and tender. Garnish with lemon crowns or radish roses.

Saginaw Bay Trout Salad

Serves: 6-8
Prep Time: 25-35 minutes

1¹/₂-2 lbs. trout fillets, cut
    into bite-sized pieces
2 T. butter or margarine
2 cups frozen corn,
    thawed
1 cup garbanzo beans,
    drained
1 4-oz. can chopped
    black olives, drained
    salt and pepper to taste

2 cans whole green
    chilis, chopped
2 green onions, chopped
¹/₃ cup fresh parsley,
    minced
¹/₄ cup oil
3 T. chicken broth
3 T. red wine vinegar
1 tsp. Dijon mustard
    lettuce leaves

In skillet, melt butter and quickly saute trout pieces for 3-5 minutes. Cover and steam for an additional 2-3 minutes or until fish flakes easily when tested with fork. Cool slightly. Combine remaining ingredients (except lettuce) in large bowl and toss gently. Spoon salad on large lettuce-lined platter.

Micro-Easy Light Sea Trout

Serves: 4
Prep Time: 20-25 minutes

4 medium sea trout, dressed
4 T. butter
1 medium onion, thinly sliced
1 lemon, sliced
    dash pepper
    parsley sprigs (optional)

Open each trout cavity and insert butter, onion, lemon and pepper. Close and secure each cavity with toothpicks. Place trout in lightly oiled non-metallic baking dish. Cover and microwave on high for 10-14 minutes or until fish flakes easily when tested with fork. Garnish with lemon slices and fresh parsley sprigs.

Sea Trout A La Delmonico

Serves: 4
Prep Time: 35-45 minutes

1	**lb. sea trout fillets**
1	**cup chicken broth**
2	**cups carrots, julienned**
1	**cup leeks (white part only), julienned**
1	**cup fennel bulb, chopped**
1	**small onion, chopped**
1/2	**tsp. salt**
1/8	**tsp. white pepper**
2	**T. butter**
1/2	**cup half-and-half**
2	**T. oil**

In medium saucepan, heat chicken broth over medium-high heat. Add carrots and leeks. Cook (covered) for 5-7 minutes or until tender; remove with slotted spoon. Place vegetables on serving platter; cover tightly with aluminum foil. Add fennel, onion, salt and pepper to broth mixture. Cook (covered) for 5 minutes. Strain, reserving broth. Discard fennel and onion. Return broth to pan and bring to a boil; reduce liquid to 1/4 cup. Over low heat, add 2 small pieces of butter at a time, whisking vigorously until melted. Repeat until all butter is used. Stir in half-and-half; cook for about 5 minutes over medium heat until mixture coats back of spoon. In skillet, add oil and cook fillets over medium-high heat for 3-4 minutes on each side or until fish flakes when tested with fork. Carefully lift fish out of pan with spatula and place on bed of vegetables. Drizzle fennel cream sauce evenly over fillets.

Priest Lake Smoke Trout

Serves: several
Prep Time: overnight plus 10-16 hours

    trout fillets
1/2 **cup rock salt**
2   **cups brown sugar**
1   **T. black pepper**
1   **T. garlic powder**
1   **T. lemon peel**

Combine all ingredients (except fish) to form dry brine. Place
single layer of fillets, skin-side down, in plastic dishpan. Cover
with brine mix. Continue to alternate fillets and brine. Chill
overnight. Rinse fillets thoroughly and pat dry with paper towels.
Air-dry fillets for 2-4 hours. Place fish, skin-side down, in smoker. Use 3 pans of wood chips and smoke for 8-12 hours or until
fillets are dark red or brown. Freeze or can smoked fish and
reheat before eating for best flavor.

Gary Brookshire
Norman, Indiana

Broiled Lake Trout

1   **lb. trout fillets**
1   **garlic clove, halved**
2   **T. olive oil**
1/4 **tsp. pepper**
4   **T. butter, melted**
1   **T. parsley, chopped**
1   **tsp. lemon juice**

Rub shallow bowl with garlic and add oil and pepper. Smear this
mixture on both sides of trout and place fish on broiling rack.
Broil 4-5 inches from heat, turning once, until fish is golden
brown and tender. Combine butter, parsley and lemon juice;
drizzle over fish.

Grilled Trout Italiano

Serves: 4
Prep Time: 45 minutes

4	**rainbow trout, boned with head removed**
2	**T. dry white wine**
2	**garlic cloves, minced**
1	**T. fresh parsley, chopped**
1	**tsp. fresh oregano, chopped**
1/4	**tsp. salt**
1/8	**tsp. ground white pepper**
2	**T. olive oil**

Combine all ingredients (except trout and oil) to form marinade. Gradually whisk in oil. Pour marinade over trout and marinate for about 30 minutes in refrigerator. (In place of marinade, 1/3 cup Italian or vinaigrette may be used.) Place trout on oiled grill and cook for about 3-4 minutes per side, gently turning once. Serve immediately.

Joseph Kozlowski
Nemacolin, Pennsylvania

Tuna Dip

Serves: several
Prep Time: 15 minutes

4	cans tuna, packed in water
2	large pkgs. cream cheese
1	large onion, grated
	juice from 2 lemons
4	eggs, boiled and grated

1	pt. mayonnaise (Miracle Whip)
	salt to taste
	Tabasco sauce
	garlic salt to taste
	paprika to taste

Combine tuna, cream cheese, onion and lemon juice. Add remaining ingredients and blend. Serve as dip with fresh vegetables or crackers.

Richard Street Jr.
Lac du Flambeau, Wisconsin

Basic Poached Tuna

Serves: 4
Prep Time: 30-35 minutes

1	lb. tuna steaks or fillets
2	cups water
2	cups white wine
1	bay leaf
2	shallots, thinly sliced
1	carrot, diced
1/2	tsp. salt

Combine water, wine, bay leaf, shallots, carrot and salt in saucepan; simmer. Arrange tuna in oblong baking pan. Pour liquid over fish, cover pan tightly with aluminum foil and bake at 400 degrees for 20 minutes or until fish is tender and flaky. Carefully remove tuna from liquid and serve hot or cold.

Micro-Easy Avocado Tuna Melt

Serves: 4 (yields 8 sandwiches)
Prep Time: 20 minutes

1/2 lb. precooked tuna	**4 bagels or hard rolls,**
3 T. mayonnaise	**sliced in halves**
1 T. chopped onion	**1 avocado, peeled,**
2 T. lemon juice	**pitted and sliced**
3/4 cup Monterey Jack cheese, shredded	

Flake precooked tuna in bowl and add mayonnaise, onion and
1 T. lemon juice; mix well. Spread tuna mixture over bagels and
place on microwavable plate. Dip avocado slices in remaining
lemon juice and arrange over tuna. Sprinkle shredded cheese
over avocado-tuna mixture and cover with waxed paper.
Microwave on high until cheese melts. Do not overcook.

Grilled Marinated Tuna With Pineapple Butter

Serves: 8
Prep Time: 2 hours, 30 minutes

6-8 tuna steaks	**pineapple, drained**
1/2 cup oil	**1 tsp. fresh mint, finely**
1/3 cup soy sauce	**chopped**
1/4 cup fresh lemon juice	**1 tsp. lemon peel, grated**
	1 garlic clove, crushed
Pineapple Butter:	**lemon wedges**
1/2 cup butter, softened	**fresh parsley sprigs**
1/2 cup canned crushed	

Arrange tuna steaks in shallow baking dish. Combine oil, soy
sauce, lemon juice, lemon peel and garlic; blend well and pour
over steaks. Cover and marinate in refrigerator for 2 hours, turning several times. Prepare barbecue grill. Drain steaks, reserving marinade. Combine pineapple-butter ingredients in separate bowl. Grill tuna until flaky. Top each steak with pineapple
butter. Garnish.

Baked Pineapple Turbot

Serves: 6
Prep Time: 35-45 minutes

6	turbot fillets
1/4	tsp. pepper
1/4	tsp. ginger
1	20-oz. can pineapple chunks, drained
1	green pepper, cut into 24 strips
	dry sherry
3	T. grated coconut flakes

Season turbot with pepper and ginger and place each fillet on 12-inch square of aluminum foil. On each fillet, place 6 pineapple chunks and 4 green-pepper strips. Generously sprinkle sherry over top. Top with 1/2 T. grated coconut per fillet. Fold up edges of foil to seal fillets in packets. Place packets on baking sheet and bake at 400 degrees for 20-30 minutes or until fish is tender and flaky.

Turbot Amandine

Serves: 6
Prep Time: 15-20 minutes

1 1/2	lbs. turbot fillets
1	T. butter
1	T. oil
1/4	cup slivered almonds
1	tsp. lemon peel, grated
2	tsp. lemon juice
	parsley
	lemon wedges

Heat butter and oil in wide skillet. Add turbot and saute for 2-3 minutes on each side. Transfer to platter and keep warm. Add almonds, lemon peel and lemon juice to skillet and saute for 1 minute. Pour sauce over fillets and garnish with parsley and lemon wedges.

Walleye Amandine

Serves: 6
Prep Time: 40 minutes

6	walleye fillets		pepper
	flour		juice from 1/2 lemon
	garlic powder	1/4	lb. butter (not
	tarragon		margarine)
	curry powder	3/4	cup slivered almonds

Dredge fillets in flour to coat. Add spices to taste. Combine lemon juice, butter and almonds in small saucepan; mix well. When butter and almonds are slightly browned, add fish to pan and cook until fillets are tender. Serve, spooning butter-almond mixture over fish.

John O'Toole
Alamo, Texas

Gravy Walleye

Serves: 4-6
Prep Time: 20 minutes

6	walleye fillets		curry powder to taste
	flour		garlic powder to taste
1/4	cup butter or margarine	1/2	cup evaporated milk
	tarragon to taste	1/2	cup cream sherry
	pepper to taste		

Roll fillets in flour to coat. Melt butter or margarine in pan. Season fish with tarragon, pepper, curry powder and garlic powder. Add seasoned fish to pan. When fillets can be pierced with fork tine, pour milk over fish to cover. Stir and simmer for about 1 minute. Add wine, stir for 1 minute and serve.

John O'Toole
Alamo, Texas

Nuked Walleye

Serves: several
Prep Time: 15 minutes

> **walleye fillets**
> **lemon-pepper seasoning to taste**
> **Lawry's seasoned salt to taste**
> **melted butter**

Place walleye fillets in shallow, microwavable dish coated with
nonstick spray. Add seasonings to fish and cover dish with plastic wrap. Microwave on high power for 3-4 minutes or longer,
depending upon thickness of fillets. Serve with melted butter.

LeRoy Geist
Glasgow, Montana

Walleye Shore Lunch

Serves: 6
Prep Time: 45 minutes

10	**walleye fillets**
1	**egg**
1	**small can evaporated milk**
	pepper to taste
	cornmeal crumbs
1/2	**lb. lard**
1	**lb. bacon**

Combine egg, milk and pepper to make batter. Dip fish fillets in
batter and roll in cornmeal crumbs to coat. Melt lard in large frying pan. Cut bacon into 3-inch pieces and fry in lard until crisp.
Serve bacon as appetizer while fish fries in bacon-flavored lard.

John O'Toole
Alamo, Texas

Walleye Fillet Dijon

Serves: 2-4
Prep Time: 20-30 minutes

4-6	walleye fillets	6	sliced mushrooms
1	onion, minced	2	cups white cooking
1-2	garlic cloves, minced		wine
	black pepper, coarsely	2	T. Dijon mustard
	ground	1	cup water
1	T. cornstarch		

Place single layer of fish fillets in frying pan. Sprinkle onion, garlic and black pepper over fillets. Add mushrooms. Combine wine and mustard, mixing thoroughly and pour sauce over warm fillets. Bring to a boil. Simmer for about 10 minutes, until fish flakes easily. Place fillets on platter. Add water to sauce in pan, thicken with cornstarch.

Paul Pirrello
Rockford, Illinois

'Spiked' Pike

Serves: 8
Prep Time: 30-40 minutes

2	lbs. walleye steaks or fillets	1/4	cup parsley, minced
		1/2	cup red wine
1	medium onion, sliced	2	T. lemon juice
1 1/2	cups mushrooms, sliced	1	tsp. fresh dill
1	cup tomatoes, chopped	1/4	tsp. lemon-pepper
1/4	hot pepper, chopped		seasoning
1/3	cup green pepper, slice		

Place onion slices in lightly oiled baking pan. Arrange fish on top of onion. Combine mushrooms, tomatoes, hot pepper, green pepper and parsley and spread over fish. Mix wine, lemon juice, dill and lemon-pepper. Pour mixture over vegetables. Cover and bake at 400 degrees for 20 minutes until fish is flaky.

Whole Steamed Fish

Serves: several
Prep Time: 1 hour, 15 minutes

2-3 lbs. walleye (whole), dressed
1¹/₂ cups water
¹/₂ cup rice wine or rice wine vinegar
       dash sesame oil
2   garlic cloves, chopped
1   T. fresh ginger, chopped
5   orange slices (thin)
       parsley sprigs
       celery leaves

Rinse fish under running water and pat dry. Sprinkle salt on both sides of fish and let stand for 30 minutes at room temperature. Make 4 deep, diagonal slashes in fish on both sides. Combine water, rice wine and sesame oil in wok. Place fish in center of wok. Sprinkle garlic and ginger over fish. Arrange orange slices in overlapping rows on top of fish. Bring water to a boil and reduce heat to medium. Cover and steam fish for 15-20 minutes and serve immediately with dipping sauce. Garnish.

Sweet Sesame Sour Dipping Sauce

Serves: several
Prep Time: 10-15 minutes

1   T. white vinegar
2   T. orange marmalade
1   tsp. soy sauce
¹/₂ tsp. oil
1   tsp. fresh ginger, chopped
1   T. toasted sesame seed

In small bowl, combine all ingredients and blend well. Serve with above walleye recipe or other fish recipes enhanced by oriental-flavored sauce.

Camper's Walleye Delight

Serves: 6
Prep Time: 15-20 minutes

> **fresh walleye fillets**
> **butter or margarine**
> **tomato slices**
> **onion slices**
> **soy sauce**
> **catsup**
> **white wine**
> **garlic salt**

Spread butter or margarine (1/4 inch thick) on large piece of aluminum foil. Lay row of walleye fillets on top. Cover with tomato and onion slices. Season to taste with soy sauce, catsup and wine. Sprinkle garlic salt lightly over top. Spread another layer of butter on tomatoes and onions. Top with second sheet of aluminum foil. Pinch sides and corners together. Grill fillets over campfire. Poke hole in aluminum to let steam out. Cook for about 15 minutes. Serve fish with remaining sauce.

Daniel Tatomer
Romulus, Michigan

'Hot' Soy Dipping Sauce

Serves: several
Prep Time: 10-15 minutes

> **3 T. cider vinegar**
> **2 T. soy sauce**
> **1 T. green onion, chopped**
> **pinch white pepper**
> **dash cayenne pepper**

In small bowl, combine all ingredients and blend well.

Meals Of The West

Best In The West

Western parts of the country are home to many piscatorial emigrants. Introduced species like searun shad, striped bass, small- and large-mouth bass, brook and brown trout or carp have, in many parts of the West, replaced native species like cutthroat and rainbow trout.

If you understand water, you will understand Western fishing. Most of the West is dry. So big reservoirs water the cities, flood the fields and, in the Northwest, provide cheap electricity for aluminum plants. The species that do well in reservoirs do well in the West. Native salmons and steelhead, riverine species like stripers and shad do not.

Some of this results from geography. New Englanders feel at home on the West Coast. Thanks to plate tectonics and the San Andreas fault, the coast drops off into the deep Pacific, leaving fine bay and inshore fishing and five kinds of salmon that run in, spawn and die. Steelhead do manage to drop back to saltwater after spawning in some cases. Most inland watersheds now run warmer than before due to logging, mining and agriculture.

Most of the West's popular cold-water species depend upon stocking. Runs of wild fish are down everywhere. Species such as sturgeon also suffer lowered numbers to the point where you have catch-and-release regulations or slot limits. Fortunately, sturgeon are now hatchery fish (thanks largely to Russian emigrant fisheries' biologists).

Ancient Fishing

Fishing the West started early. Some Indians used deer sinew lines to catch salmon in prehistoric times, and more used redwood nets and spears to snare salmon. Spanish fishermen caught fish off the Pacific Coast at least 100 years before the Pilgrims stepped off onto their disappointingly small rock. Even Lewis and Clark fished during the winter of 1805 and 1806 as government records show a requisition for tackle. Salmon, steelhead, sturgeon, cutthroat and even surf smelt came in great numbers.

Mountain men did, of course, tickle trout—an old English poaching method of catching trout by hand. Settlers ate fish when they could pitchfork or hand-line them.

'Can'fusion

Even thougn a small salmon drying operation started at the mouth of the Columbia River in the 1830s, nobody bothered much with Western fishing until after the Civil War.

War-spawned technological change brought canning as a means of feeding soldiers in the field. Suddenly, the salmon that Westerners saw as something to pitchfork out of creeks to feed hogs (and a nuisance that stunk up streams after the spawning runs) had value. Once the railroads punched through the Sierras and Cascades, a market developed for trout: to feed passengers. This just about cleaned out fisheries like Lake Tahoe. Then, too, you could ice and ship trout to both coasts.

It's interesting that Captain Josua Slocum, first to sail solo around the world, helped design the sailing trollers that started to supplement gill netters after the turn of the century. This, when fishermen discovered hooked fish fetched more at the market than those mashed in nets.

The California Connection

About this time men from the East, and the local pre-yuppies that also founded the Sierra Club, started fishing in the Sierras. The "return to nature" movement largely fueled urbanites with disposable incomes and the desire to emulate the "proper British" sportsman to become a new generation of fishermen. Given the primitive state of reels until the Southern baitcasters organized, fly fishing was the method of choice inland. Many methods, such as coho flies, came through Canada where displaced chalk stream anglers fished out the day in tweeds.

Salmon, trout and steelhead were the fish of choice for the upscale angler and the Indians. Not many fished for the black bass introduced into deltas and the increasing number of reservoirs that barred spawning streams.

Slumming For Shad

"Bumping" shad by running an outboard in delta waters while holding a net behind the motor had its fans. But most shad were caught in gill nets and turned into pet food. Only after World War II, when another burst of war-fueled technology brought monofilament line, fiberglass rods and spinning tackle, did shad become a usual quarry of the sportfisherman. In the 1940s and 1950s, 100 shad-to-net days were common enough to be boring. Today, 20 shad to net deserve applause. Such is the state of shad.

Striper Spreading

Striped bass, which were introduced (like shad) by a series of small stockings from train-engine water tanks in the 1800s, had spread from the California delta country to Oregon and beyond. In salmon country, stripers were considered trash fish to dump on the bank. In California, bay and delta striper fishermen hammered fish from their spawning rivers into the bay and out to ocean beaches. As late as the 1940s, few experts kept fish under 20 pounds and 100-pound limits were easy.

As technology improved results, and the number of fishermen with boats, depthfinders, decent gear and leisure time increased both as a percentage of the population and in raw numbers, striper numbers declined. Some blamed this on the delta project. In Oregon, they blamed the problem on water quality. Overall, it's clear that stripers can tolerate lower water quality than salmon or steelhead, but they can't, even with stocking projects, survive the pumps that send northern California water south and year-round angler predation.

Landlocked Stripers

Stripers are even hurting in reservoirs. In Nevada impoundments, for example, the same water clearing that has turned the Colorado River into a trout stream has reduced the size of the food pyramid to a point that local anglers have tried things like spraying fertilizer on the water; however, they have had only limited success. Only in reservoirs stocked with water pumped out from the delta through the Central Valley Project do stripers seem to thrive.

Trout Time

Trout manage. The lovely golden trout of the Sierras now seem safe in their natal waters near Mt. Whitney. More have been shipped to states like Wyoming where they grow to larger sizes in remote waters.

Other rainbow species seem to be doing fine, and new management and feeding techniques ensure an indefinite supply of "truck trout" for the road-bound angler who is satisfied with cigar-sized rainbows. Stocking programs and catch-and-release continue throughout the West. Clearly catch-and-release allows more to enjoy the fish. It's not clear how heavy catch-and-release pressures affect trout numbers.

Better Brookies

Even brook trout seem on the upswing. Even though they require colder water that trout (other than lakers), they can spawn without current; therefore, they are the choice for alpine lakes. Early stocks from rather inferior quick maturing lines that rapidly overpopulate many waters are now being replaced by bigger, slower-to-mature trout from Canadian stock.

Lagging Lake And Bull Trout

Lake trout are easily available in Canada, and they don't seem as happy in the United States. Lake Tahoe lakers, as well as those in most other waters, grow smaller each year.

Part of this is due to improved depthfinding and deep-trolling methods. In some waters, pollution and warming from development, agriculture and logging seem to be the cause of declines in both size and numbers. In most cases, increased fishing pressure compounds the problem.

Dolly Varden, or bull trout, are rapidly approaching endangered status in many parts of the West. These colorful trout have a limited range and rather particular habitat requirement. Sea-run Dollies, a great light tackle fish, may do a bit better than other species because they spend time offshore.

Big Bad Browns

Brown trout, both the Scottish loch still-water varieties and the moving water types from Germany, do better than most anglers expect. Browns are smarter, more durable and better able to tolerate higher temperatures than other trout. They thrive in tailwaters and in deep reservoirs.

Brown populations do vary over time. When first stocked in reservoirs with large numbers of baitfish they grow fast to become a dominant age class. Flaming Gorge, for example, was extremely hot for browns and Bob Bringenhurst's long-time record came from there. However, the biggest browns today seem to come from the Midwestern tailwaters with uniform temperatures and perfect conditions, allowing them to grow year-round.

Western fishermen should note that striped bass-size plugs 6 to 9 inches long and finished to match trout are successful in catching very large browns.

Warm Water, Tepid Interest

Bass, crappie, bluegills, catfish and other warm-water species collected more ethnic slurs than angling interest until the post-World War II anglers discovered you didn't need to shovel snow all winter in the West. Prior to that, most of the above species had reputations equivalent to carp. Smallmouth bass were a bit of an exception because they thrived in reasonably scenic streams in "pointy tree" country. Walleyes, now almost endemic to the Columbia Basin and available in all Western states (except Alaska and Hawaii), attract increased interest, too; however, the boom on the Columbia has slowed.

Today, of course, thousands of warm-water reservoirs impound Western waters and the river deltas where the number of salmon, steelhead and stripers are low enough to require punch cards and low limits. These reservoirs are experiencing angling pressure. Most are close to home, so anglers make do with warm-water species. Reservoirs are the primary in-close fishing option for most fishermen.

Catfish, carp and other oddments, such as the Sacramento River perch or whitefish, offer an option worth considering. It's agreed that a nice channel catfish from a decent free-stone stream is more attractive than a truck trout raised on cat food in a concrete trough.

Hula Land Happenings

Hawaii offers the world's most convenient gamefishing. Boats leave the big island to troll the sheltered waters off the Kona Coast. However, there's solid inshore action from rocks, and, if you can figure out the morass of regulations, reef fishing for the bigger brothers of aquarium fish.

Largemouth and peacock bass abound in inland reservoirs, a couple of rivers and farm ponds. Add a variety of Chinese catfish that hits plugs plus, on Kauai, rainbow trout in a rain forest, and there's plenty happening.

California Classics
Serves: 4-6

You might enjoy this menu in a fine Monterey, California, water-front restaurant as you watch sea otters napping in the kelp.

Soup: Squid Chowder

1	lb. fresh or frozen squid	3	T. flour
2	cups water	3	cups milk
4	bacon slices or 1/2 pound		salt and pepper
	salt pork		dillweed
1	medium onion, chopped		
2	potatoes, diced into 1/2-inch cubes		

Clean and skin squid. Cover squid with water and simmer for 35 minutes or until tender. Drain squid and reserve liquid, adding enough water to make 2 cups liquid (if needed). Finely chop squid. Cut bacon or salt pork into 1/4-inch cubes and brown in saucepan with onion until soft. Add reserved liquid and potatoes. Cover and cook until tender. Mix flour with 1/2 cup milk until smooth; add to potato mixture. Bring to a boil, stirring constantly; reduce heat. Add remaining milk and squid. Heat thoroughly (do not boil). Season with salt and pepper to taste. Garnish with dillweed and serve. (Note: In Monterey, they serve this chowder on hollowed-out, 5-inch-diameter French bread loaves. This option works with any quality bread.)

Entree: Lingcod Nicoise

2	lbs. lingcod fillets (or 4-lb. whole bass)
1/4	cup olive oil
3	garlic cloves, minced
1	T. tomato paste
1	cup white wine
1	T. parsley flakes
1	tsp. thyme or Italian seasoning
1/8	tsp. salt
1/4	tsp. pepper
1	cup pitted black olives

In small saucepan, heat oil and add garlic. Saute gently for 30 seconds. Add tomato paste, wine, parsley, thyme, salt and pepper. Bring to a boil over medium heat and cook for 3 minutes. Remove from heat and cool. In baking dish, lay fillets in single layer. (If using whole fish, cut 3 slashes 1/4 inch thick about 2 inches apart on top of fish and lay fish in dish.) Spoon three-fourths of sauce over fillets (or fish) and bake at 350 degrees for 10 minutes. (Bake for 30 minutes if using whole fish.) Add olives and baste with remaining tomato sauce. Continue to cook fish for 10 minutes or until fish flakes when tested with fork.

Salad: Fettuccini With Gorgonzola Sauce

- 1 **lb. spinach fettuccini**
- 3/4 **cup dry white wine**
- 1 **cup heavy cream**
- 4 **oz. Gorgonzola cheese, crumbled**
- 2 **T. Parmesan cheese**
- 1 **T. Romano cheese**
- 1 **T. chopped fresh basil**

Cook fettuccini according to package directions. Prepare sauce: In small saucepan, heat wine and cook for 4 minutes over medium heat. Add cream and bring to a boil; then lower heat. Add Gorgonzola cheese and continue to simmer for 15 minutes. Add Parmesan and Romano cheeses. Stir in basil. Remove from heat and toss with fettuccini. Serve with more Parmesan cheese and ground black pepper.

Dessert: Coffee Nut Tortoni

- 1 **cup heavy cream**
- 6 **T. sugar**
- 1 **T. instant coffee**
- 1 **tsp. vanilla**
- 1/2 **tsp. almond extract**
- 1 **egg white**
- 1/4 **cup toasted almonds, finely chopped**
- 1/4 **cup toasted coconut, flaked**
  maraschino cherries (optional)

Whip cream and fold in 4 T. sugar, coffee, vanilla and almond extract. Beat egg white until soft peaks form; gradually add remaining 2 T. sugar and beat until stiff peaks form. Mix almonds and coconut together. Fold egg white into whipped cream and half of almond-coconut mixture. Place paper cupcake liners in muffin pan and fill with tortoni. Sprinkle top with remaining almond-coconut mixture; freeze until firm. Top with maraschino cherries.

Oregon Offerings
Serves: 4-6

Portland manages the charm of San Francisco or Seattle with reasonable traffic and some of the best clamming, tidewater and ocean fishing, as well as stream action, in the West. Food here features ocean delights like smelt, clams (one restaurant has its own private leased clam beds!), crabs, salmon and steelhead. Add mussels and other marine edibles and only a classic Mediterranean cioppino can let you sample everything in one sitting. This meal's entree isn't the "neatest" dish to eat, so the Sticky Smelt finger-lickin' appetizer will get you off to a good start! Few can manage heavy desserts with this menu, so consider a fresh ginger fruit.

Appetizer: Sticky Smelt

2	lbs. smelt
1/4	cup flour
1/2	cup oil
1/2	cup soy sauce
1/3	cup sugar
3	tsp. fresh ginger root, grated
1	tsp. garlic powder
1	T. roasted sesame seeds

Clean smelt by twisting heads gently as you pull to remove heads and entrails together. Rinse in cold water and pat dry. Dust with flour. Heat oil in skillet over medium heat and fry smelt until crisp on both sides. Combine soy sauce, sugar, ginger and garlic powder in separate pan or skillet and heat, stirring until sugar dissolves. Add smelt and spoon glaze over fish. Cook over low heat until fish glaze and liquid evaporate. Sprinkle

sesame seeds over top of fish and serve. (Note: Most fresh- and
saltwater panfish and small trout can substitute for smelt in this
recipe. Clean small panfish and trout in your usual manner. Eat
with your fingers and watch for bones.)

Entree: Mediterranean Fish Cioppino

3	lbs. cod, bass or perch
3	lbs. fresh shellfish (crab, clams, mussels or crayfish)
1/2	lb. fresh shrimp or prawns
6	T. olive oil
2	large onions, chopped
3	garlic cloves, minced
1	cup of red wine
1/2	cup water
1	1-lb. can stewed tomatoes, chopped
1	bay leaf
2	T. fresh parsley
1	tsp. rosemary leaves
1/2	tsp. salt
1/4	tsp. pepper
	French bread

Clean, scale and cut fish into 2-inch chunks. Crack crablegs and
scrub clams and/or mussels. Remove shells from shrimp,
prawns and/or crayfish. Heat oil in large saucepan over low heat.
Saute onions and garlic until golden brown. Stir in wine, water,
tomatoes, bay leaf, parsley, rosemary, salt and pepper. Cook for
15 minutes over medium heat. Add fish and shellfish and simmer for 10-20 minutes or until fish flakes and crab turns red; discard any shellfish with shells that do not open. Place thick slice
of French bread in each soup bowl and serve cioppino on top.
(Note: Shells may be left on shrimp to enhance flavor.)

Dessert: Ginger Fruit

1	orange	1	pink grapefruit
1	red apple	5	T. coconut
1	green apple	2-3	T. crystallized ginger,
2	bananas		slivered

Peel or cut fruit into bite-sized pieces. Mix fruit with coconut and ginger. Chill for 20 minutes and serve.

Washington Wildfare
Serves: 4-6

While Seattle and Tacoma summers remain temperate, you can try this "east of the Cascades" cool-summer menu, which keeps the cook and diners from frying. The highlight of this wonderful spread is the Dungeness crab, the West Coast's version of New England lobster. Add a good bread to sop up excess crabmeat and juice from the big serving bowl.

Appetizer: Smoked Trout Dip

1	cup smoked trout, flaked	2	tsp. chopped chives
		2	tsp. onion juice
1/2	cup mayonnaise	1/4	tsp. dillweed
1	cup sour cream	1/8	tsp. pepper
2	T. lemon juice		paprika

Skin, bone and flake smoked trout. Combine ingredients (except paprika) in small bowl and chill for 2 hours. Sprinkle paprika over top and serve with celery and carrot sticks or crackers, toast or chips.

Salad: Black Cod And Mandarin Orange Salad

2	lbs. black cod, filleted or steaked
1	small yellow onion, chopped
6	peppercorns, chopped
1/2	cup celery, finely chopped
1	6½-oz. can mandarin oranges, drained
1/2	cup roasted almonds, sliced

1   **small red onion, sliced**
1/2   **cup creamy onion salad dressing**
1/8   **tsp. salt**
1/8   **tsp. pepper**
1   **bunch spinach**

Cover cod fillets with water and add yellow onion and pepper-corn; poach for 15 minutes over medium heat or until fish flakes when tested with fork. Drain and cool. Then flake fish and remove bones. Combine fish flakes with celery, mandarin oranges, almonds, red onion and salad dressing. Add salt and pepper and mix well. Tear spinach leaves, remove stems and make spinach bed. Scoop cod mixture on top and serve.

Entree: Dressed Dungeness Crab

2   **fresh Dungeness crabs, cooked**

Dressing:
2   **T. red wine garlic vinegar**
3   **T. lemon juice**
1/2   **tsp. salt**
1/2   **tsp. pepper**
6   **T. olive oil**
1   **T. oregano or basil leaves**
1   **tsp. garlic powder**

Crack crablegs and pinchers so each remains attached to part of crab body. Make sure to keep crab liver (yellow contents of upper shell). Blend crab liver with dressing ingredients. Pour dressing over crabs and refrigerate for at least 2 hours, turning every 3 minutes.

Dessert: Cream Cheese Berry Pie

Pastry Crust:
1   **cup plus 2 T. flour**   1/2   **tsp. salt**
5   **T. shortening**   4   **T. ice cold water**

Filling:

3	cups berries (boysenberry, blueberry, blackberry)	6	oz. cream cheese, softened
1/2	cup sugar	1	cup whipped cream
2	tsp. cornstarch		
6	T. Creme de Cassis liqueur		

Combine flour, shortening and salt in bowl; mix until well-blended and pieces are pea-sized. Add 1 T. ice-cold water at a time until dough forms into ball. Wrap dough in waxed paper and chill for 20 minutes. On floured surface, roll pastry dough to fit 9-inch pie plate. Crimp edges with fork and poke holes on bottom and sides of pie crust. Bake at 400 degrees for 25 minutes or until golden brown. Cool.

For filling, clean berries and set aside 1 cup whole berries. In saucepan, add remaining 2 cups berries and mash. Add sugar and cornstarch and bring to a boil over medium heat for 5 minutes. Add 3 T. liqueur and cook for 1 minute more. Remove from heat and cool. Beat cream cheese with remaining 3 T. liqueur until smooth; spread on bottom of cooled pie shell. Place whole berries on cream cheese, pour cooled berry mixture on top and spread. Refrigerate for 4 hours. Top with whipped cream.

Alaskan Abundance

Serves: 4-6

Clams, salmon, halibut and a host of other fish make Alaska a choice spot for fish fanciers. None of these fish species need fancy "fixings" to make a great meal. A simple salad and a baked potato work well. Those who insist on dessert can dip strawberries into sour cream and brown sugar and pop them into their mouths.

Appetizer: Clam And Spinach Canapes

1	10-oz. pkg. frozen spinach
2	T. butter
1	7 1/2-oz. can minced clams, drained
1/2	tsp. lemon-pepper seasoning

12   **bread slices (white)**
2   **T. grated Parmesan cheese**

Cook spinach according to package directions; drain, squeeze dry and chop. Add chopped spinach to melted butter and cook over medium heat until liquid evaporates. Remove from heat. Stir in minced clams and lemon-pepper seasoning; mix well. Trim crusts from bread and cut bread into squares. Toast both sides of bread squares under broiler. Spread clam mixture onto bread squares, sprinkle cheese over top and return to broiler. Brown before serving.

Soup: Salmon Chowder

2   **cups leftover salmon, flaked or 1-lb. can**
2   **cups water**
1   **cup tomato juice**
1/4   **cup onion, chopped**
1   **cup potatoes, diced into 1/2-inch cubes**
1/2   **cup celery, chopped**
4   **T. butter**
4   **T. flour**
1   **tsp. salt**
1   **tsp. parsley flakes**
1   **tsp. dry mustard**
2 1/2   **cups milk**
3   **drops Worcestershire sauce**
1   **T. dry sherry**

Combine salmon, water, tomato juice, onion, potatoes and celery in saucepan and simmer for 40 minutes. Melt butter in separate saucepan and add flour, salt, parsley and mustard. Mix until smooth; then slowly add milk. Cook over medium heat while stirring until sauce thickens. Combine with salmon mixture and add Worcestershire sauce and sherry. Serve immediately.

Entree: Grilled Halibut With Biggie Butter

1 1/2   **lbs. halibut steaks**   **1/2**   **tsp. garlic powder**
1/2   **cup oil**   **1/8**   **tsp. salt**
3   **T. lemon juice**   **1/8**   **tsp. pepper**
1   **tsp. tarragon leaves**

Lemon Butter:

1/4	cup butter	1	tsp. catsup
	grated rind from 1 lemon	1	tsp. dillweed

Rinse halibut steaks and pat dry. Combine oil, lemon juice, tarragon, garlic powder, salt and pepper. Pour marinade over fish and refrigerate for 3 minutes; drain. Cook fish over grill at moderate heat. Baste with marinade. To make lemon butter, soften butter and mix with other ingredients. Chill until ready to serve with halibut.

Vancouver—The Other Indian's Food

Serves: 4-6

Vancouver seems an increasingly popular retirement community for those in the diplomatic service, so it should be no surprise that, aside from the wonderful Chinese food, Indian and other ethnic restaurants abound. This menu features Indian classics from the old world.

Appetizer: Chutney Eggs

6   **eggs**
3   **T. chutney**
4   **tsp. milk**
1   **T. roasted almonds**

Hard boil eggs and cool. Peel eggs and split eggs in halves; remove yolks and reserve whites. Mash egg yolks with milk. Stir in chutney. Fill egg whites with chutney-yolk mixture. Top with roasted almonds. (Note: This recipe can be made a day ahead and refrigerated until needed.)

Entree: Tandoori Salmon

6-8   **salmon steaks**
3   **tsp. Sharwood's Tandoori Mix**

2 **T. plain yogurt**
1¹/₂ **T. white wine vinegar**
2 **T. fresh lemon juice**
2 **T. vegetable oil**

Combine tandoori mix, yogurt, vinegar, lemon juice and oil in small bowl. In large shallow baking dish, place fish in single layer and sprinkle 3 T. lemon juice over top. Spread tandoori marinade over salmon steaks to coat evenly. Cover dish with plastic wrap and let marinate overnight, turning once or twice. Remove steaks and grill over gray charcoal or broil 4-6 inches from grill (moderate heat) for about 10 minutes per side or until fish flakes when tested with fork. Make sure to separate charcoal for a cooler fire so fish will cook before coating chars. (Note: Several companies make tandoori mix. Sharwood's Tandoori Mix tastes great and is available in most gourmet shops or by mail order. You can also find directions to make your own mix in Indian cookbooks.)

Side Dish No.1: Pilaf With Curry Dressing

2 **T. butter**
2 **T. oil**
1 **small onion, chopped**
1 **cup long grain rice**
2 **cups chicken broth or water**
3 **T. chopped dry apricots**
3 **T. golden raisins**
3 **T. roasted almonds**
2 **T. lemon juice**

Curry Dressing:
¹/₂ **cup plain yogurt**
3 **T. sour cream**
2 **T. chopped green onion (fresh)**
1 **small garlic clove, minced**
¹/₈ **tsp. dry mustard**
¹/₈ **tsp. ground ginger**
1 **tsp. mild curry powder**
1 **T. chopped green-onion stems (fresh)**

In skillet, melt butter with 1 T. oil over medium heat. Add onion and lightly brown. Stir in rice and cook until transparent. Add broth and bring to a boil. Lower heat to simmer, cover and cook for 18 minutes or until liquid is absorbed. Toss with fork and add apricots, raisins, almonds, lemon juice and remaining oil. Refrigerate. (Note: Individual pilaf servings can be molded in foam plastic cups. Run a knife around cup edge and pilaf will loosen, then place on lettuce, top with curry dressing, garnish with egg halves and serve.)

To make dressing, combine all ingredients in small bowl and refrigerate for 30 minutes or longer. (Note: This cool dressing also goes nicely on grilled fish and summer salads. It keeps up to a week in the refrigerator. It's rather mild so you might like to add more curry powder or, if a convicted "chili head," 1 or more hot red peppers!)

Side Dish No.2: Pita Rounds

**1   pita bread loaf
    butter or margarine**

Indians serve pan and other flat breads with meals. An easy alternative is pita bread, which has become increasingly available in stores. Heat your oven to 350 degrees, brush bread with melted butter or margarine and warm. Cut bread into quarters and serve.

Dessert: Lime Ice

**1   cup sugar
4   cups cold water
1   cup lime juice
2   drops green food coloring
8-10   mint leaves (optional)**

In saucepan, boil sugar with water until dissolved. Lower heat and simmer for 8 minutes; cool. Stir in lime juice and food coloring. Pour mixture into ice-cube trays. Cover trays tightly with plastic wrap or foil and freeze until barely firm. Before serving, beat with fork until slushy and fill chilled sherbet dishes or wine glasses. (Note: Lime dessert won't keep more than 24 hours.)

Hawaii Chinese-Style

Serves: 4

This oriental dinner makes a colorful and tasty dinner that stresses the loving attention to texture and appearance in Hawaiian cooking. When steaming in a bamboo or other steamer, the plate holding your food must be 3/4- to 1-inch smaller in diameter than the steam container. This lets steam rise around the dish and cook the contents. You should realize that a wok and bamboo steamer are not vital for this type of cooking, although both are convenient and traditional. A Dutch oven with a wire rack placed above boiling-water level also works. Just cut food to uniform thickness to steam evenly and use thin cuts of fish or other foods that steam faster than chunks. Try thick, thin and dark soy sauce, as well as hoisin and black-bean sauces. These make a lot of difference if you want an authentic taste.

Entree: Chinese Lemon Fish

2	lbs. fish fillets
1/2	lemon, sliced

Coating:

1	large egg white	1	T. cornstarch
1/2	tsp. salt	1/2	T. vegetable oil
1	T. sherry or white wine		

Sauce:

1	T. thin soy sauce	1	tsp. sugar
2	tsp. black-bean sauce	2	tsp. lemon juice
1	T. hoisin sauce	1/2	tsp. grated lemon peel
1	T. sherry	1	T. vegetable oil

If fillets are thick, slice into 1/2-inch slices. Cut lemon into 1/8-inch-thick slices, then cut each slice in half. With fork, beat egg white until gel is broken. In bowl, add fish and stir in egg white. Stir in salt and sherry; add cornstarch and mix well. Then add 1 T. oil and mix until smooth. Chill coated fillets uncovered in refrigerator for 30-40 minutes to set coating.

Combine all sauce ingredients in bowl; mix well. (Soy sauce can be substituted for black-bean and hoisin sauces if needed.)

Spread coated fillets evenly into 8- to 9-inch pie plate; cover with sauce ingredients. Place lemon slices on top. In wok or other steamer, add enough water to come just below rim of steamer or rack. Bring to a boil over high heat. Place plate with fish on steamer, cover and steam over medium-high heat for 20 minutes or until fish flakes. Add more boiling water to wok if necessary to prevent drying out. Serve over shallow-fried noodles.

Broccoli Flowerettes With Black Bean Sauce

- 1 **small bunch broccoli**
- 1 **T. fermented black beans (heaping)**
- 3 **T. oil**
- 1 **garlic clove, minced**
- 1/2 **tsp. fresh ginger, minced**
- 1/2 **tsp. salt**
- 1/2 **tsp. sugar**
- 1/2 **cup vegetable broth**

Thickener:
- 1 1/2 **tsp. cornstarch**
- 3 **T. water**
- 1 **tsp. sesame or cooking oil**

Break off broccoli flowerettes. Rinse fermented black beans in water, shake dry and chop. Heat wok or heavy iron frying pan over high heat. Add oil, swirl and heat for 30 seconds. Add black beans, garlic and ginger; stir for 20 seconds. Add broccoli flowerettes, stir and flip for 20 seconds. Lower heat to medium and continue to stir for about 2 minutes. Add salt, sugar and broth; stir and cover. Steam cook for 2 minutes. Combine thickener ingredients. Uncover wok, stir in cornstarch mixture. Cook until sauce thickens (about 30 seconds). Serve immediately.

Dessert: Macadamia Nut Chocolate Chip Cookies

- 1/2 **cup brown sugar**
- 1 **cup granulated sugar**
- 1/2 **lb. butter, softened**

1	tsp. pure vanilla extract
2	eggs
2	cups flour
1	tsp. baking soda
1	tsp. salt
1¹/₂	cups semi-sweet chocolate chips
1	cup macadamia nuts (pieces are best)

Preheat oven to 350 degrees. Beat sugars and butter until fluffy and light. Add vanilla and eggs; beat. Combine flour, soda and salt; add to above batter and stir well. Add chips and nuts. Grease cookie sheets. Form cookies a tablespoon at a time and cook for about 10 minutes. Let cool for 5 minutes on cookie sheet, then remove to racks with sharp edge spatula. (Tip: Center of cookies should be soft; edges brown.)

Recipes For:

Whitefish

Whiting

Your Choice Of Fish

Stuffed Whitefish

Serves: 4
Prep Time: 2 hours, 20 minutes

- **2 large whitefish (with heads)**
- **1 pkg. dry stuffing mix (pork flavor)**
- **juice from 1 lemon**
- **1/8 cup water**
- **1/4 tsp. ground garlic**
- **1/4 tsp. ground white pepper**
- **1 bunch parsley**
- **1 large lemon, sliced**

Prepare stuffing according to package directions. Add lemon juice and water. Sprinkle garlic, pepper and half of parsley into fish cavities. Add remaining lemon juice to prepared stuffing. Top fish with lemon slices and remaining parsley. Wrap fish in aluminum foil and place on large cookie sheet. Bake at 250 degrees for 1 1/2-2 hours. Flavor is enhanced by slow cooking.

Dean Auger
Gladstone, Michigan

Milk-Poached Whitefish

Serves: 4
Prep Time: 20-30 minutes

- **1 1/2 lbs. whitefish fillets**
- **3 cups milk**
- **1 cup sour cream**
- **1 T. dried minced onion**
- **2 T. butter, melted**
- **2 hard-boiled eggs, chopped**
- **1 T. fresh parsley, minced**

In small bowl, combine milk, sour cream, onion and melted butter. Place fish in buttered baking dish and pour sauce over fish. Bake at 400 degrees for 10 minutes or until fish is flaky when tested with fork. Combine chopped eggs and parsley and sprinkle over fish fillets before serving.

Quick Fish

Serves: 2
Prep Time: 15 minutes

- **2** **whitefish, cut into 2-inch squares**
  cornmeal
- **1/4** **T. orange peel**
- **1/4** **T. lemon peel**
  java pepper to taste
  garlic salt to taste
  shortening

Combine cornmeal, orange and lemon peel, java pepper and garlic salt. Roll fish in mixture or put mixture and fish into bag and shake. Fry in shortening or fat until crisp. (Flavor is better if fried quickly in heavy frying pan or deep-fat fryer.)

Donald Warren
Lompoc, California

Great Lakes Special

Serves: 8
Prep Time: 45-50 minutes

- **1** **cup whitefish, cooked and flaked**
- **1** **green pepper, chopped**
- **2** **tsp. capers**
- **1** **cup celery, chopped**
- **3** **green onions (with tops), diced**
- **1** **cup dry bread cubes**
- **3** **T. Italian salad dressing mix**
- **1** **cup cottage cheese**
- **1/2** **cup cheddar cheese, shredded**

Combine all ingredients (except cheddar cheese), folding cottage cheese in last. Place mixture in buttered casserole and top with cheddar cheese. Bake at 350 degrees for 25-30 minutes.

Whole Grilled Whitefish With Lime-Mint Butter

Serves: 6-8
Prep Time: 30-45 minutes

1   **3-8-lb. whitefish (whole), cleaned, gutted
    and scaled with head and tail removed
    cooking oil
    freshly ground black pepper**
1   **tsp. grated lime peel**
3   **limes, thinly sliced**

Lime-Mint Butter:
1   **cup butter, softened**
1/4 **tsp. ginger (optional)**
3   **T. lime juice**
1/2 **tsp. grated lime rind**
1/2-1 **tsp. mint leaves, finely chopped**

Brush fish cavity with oil and season with pepper and lime peel. Overlap lime slices in fish cavity. Oil fish thoroughly. Place fish in oiled fish basket. Cook 4-6 inches from banked coals (covered) allowing 10-12 minutes per inch of thickness. Baste occasionally. Turn fish and oil grill again halfway through cooking time. Cook fish until flaky when tested with fork. To prepare lime-mint butter, cream ingredients together and spread over cooked fish. Serve immediately.

Portuguese Whiting (Hake)

Serves: 4-6
Prep Time: 45-55 minutes

4-6 whiting (hake) fillets
1/8 tsp. pepper
1 onion, finely chopped
1 garlic clove, minced
1/4 cup parsley
1 fresh thyme sprig or
1 tsp. dried thyme
3 tomatoes, peeled, seeded and chopped
1/2 cup white wine
1/4 tsp. salt

Season fish with pepper and place in wide skillet. Add remaining ingredients and bring to a boil. Reduce heat and simmer (covered) for 10 minutes. Carefully remove fish and keep warm. Continue to cook tomato mixture for 5 minutes then pour over fish and serve immediately.

Micro-Easy Yogurt Fish Fillets

Serves: 4-6
Prep Time: 20-30 minutes

2 lbs. whiting (hake) fillets
1 cup plain yogurt
2 T. scallions, chopped
1 T. lemon juice

1 T. parsley, chopped
1 T. chives, chopped
1 T. sweet red pepper, chopped

Place fish fillets in large, greased, shallow, non-metallic baking dish. Combine remaining ingredients and spread over fillets. Cover with vented plastic wrap. Microwave on high for 7-8 minutes or until fish begins to flake when tested with fork. Turn dish and microwave an additional 2-3 minutes on high. Remove and let stand (covered) for 4-5 minutes.

Stuffed Hake Fillets

Serves: 8
Prep Time: 45 minutes

2	lbs. skinless hake fillets	4	tsp. parsley, chopped
2	tsp. oil	1/2	tsp. Italian seasonings
1/4	cup onion, finely chopped	1/2	tsp. garlic powder
1/4	cup celery, chopped	1/8	tsp. pepper
2	cups soft bread crumbs	1	T. margarine, melted

Heat oil in small saucepan and add onion and celery, cooking and stirring until tender. Stir in bread crumbs, 3 tsp. parsley, Italian seasonings, garlic powder and pepper. Arrange half of fillets in shallow, lightly oiled baking pan and spread bread mixture over fillets. Top with remaining fillets. Cover and bake at 400 degrees for 15-20 minutes. Mix melted margarine with remaining parsley and pour over fillets. Uncover and bake for 5 more minutes or until fish flakes easily.

Baked Whiting With Capers

Serves: 4
Prep Time: 30-40 minutes

1	2-lb. whiting, dressed	1	tsp. fresh parsley, chopped
5	T. butter		
1/8	tsp. pepper	1	tsp. fresh chives, chopped
1/8	tsp. nutmeg		
2	T. capers	2	tsp. lemon juice

Combine 2 T. butter, pepper, nutmeg and capers; rub mixture over whiting. Place fish in baking dish, cover and bake at 350 degrees for 20-25 minutes or until fish is flaky and tender. Melt 3 T. butter in saucepan and add remaining ingredients. Pour caper sauce over fish before serving.

Classic Grilled Whiting

Serves: 6
Prep Time: 50-60 minutes

6	whiting steaks or large fillets	1/4	tsp. grated lime peel
1/4	cup oil	2	tsp. dried basil
1/4	cup lime juice	1/4	cup green onion, chopped
	salt and pepper to taste		

Rinse, pat dry and place whiting steaks in glass baking dish. Combine oil, lime juice, lime peel, basil and green onion to make marinade. Mix well and pour marinade over fish, marinating for 30 minutes. Season fish with salt and pepper. Remove fish and place on moderately hot grill in oiled fish basket. Cook (uncovered) for 2-3 minutes to sear fish. Then cover with lid or foil tent. (Allow 10 minutes cooking time per inch of fish.) Cook fish until flaky when tested with fork. Baste with lime marinade.

Cape Cod Salad

Serves: 4-6
Prep Time: 30-40 minutes

2	cups whiting, cooked and flaked	1/4	cup zucchini, thinly sliced
2	cups head lettuce, shredded	1/2	cup carrots, grated
3	cups mixed lettuce, shredded	1/2	cup mayonnaise
1/2	cup red onions, sliced	1/2	cup plain yogurt
1/2	cup green pepper rings	1	tsp. horseradish
1	pt. cherry tomatoes	2	tsp. fresh dill, minced
			salt and pepper to taste

Combine lettuce, onions, green pepper, zucchini and carrots; toss. Place fish evenly on top of salad greens in serving bowl. In separate bowl, combine mayonnaise, yogurt, horseradish, dill and salt and pepper. Pour dressing over fish and garnish with tomatoes.

Molded Fish Fillets

Serves: 6
Prep Time: 45 minutes

> 2   **lbs. fish fillets cut into serving-sized pieces**
>   **salt and pepper to taste**
> 1   **cup onion, sliced**
> 1   **pkg. unflavored gelatin**
> 1/4   **cup cold water**
> 1   **16-oz. can chicken broth**
>   **lemons, thinly sliced**
>   **olives, thinly slices**

Sour Cream Sauce:
> 1   **cup sour cream**
> 1/4   **tsp. prepared mustard**
> 1   **tsp. onion, grated**
> 1   **tsp. parsley, chopped**
>   **juice from 1/2 lemon**

Season fish with salt and pepper. Place onion on bottom of baking dish and put fish on top. Bake at 350 degrees for 30 minutes or until fish flakes easily. Cool. Soften gelatin in cold water. Heat chicken broth and add to gelatin mixture. Chill until gelatin starts to thicken. Put half of gelatin on deep platter and add fish on top of gelatin. Garnish with lemon slices and olives. Combine sour cream, mustard, onion, parsley and lemon juice to make sauce. Chill and serve with fish.

Robert Seidles
Downey, Indiana

Oven-Smoked Fish

Serves: 10
Prep Time: overnight plus 5 hours, 30 minutes

3-4   **lbs. fish fillets**
1¹/₂   **cups salt**
²/₃   **cup brown sugar**
¹/₂   **cup soy sauce**
1   **medium onion, grated**
1   **T. pepper**
    juice from 1 lemon
    liquid smoke

Spread:
  8   **oz. light cream cheese**
  2   **tsp. lemon juice**
    garlic to taste
    paprika to taste

Combine salt, brown sugar, soy sauce, onion, pepper and lemon juice; spread mixture on fillets. Place fish in covered container to cure overnight (14-24 hours). Then rinse fish in cold water to remove mixture. Place fish on cookie sheet covered with aluminum foil. Generously shake liquid smoke on fish. Cover with foil and bake at 200 degrees for 5 hours. Cool fish before storing. Wrap fillets individually in plastic wrap and put in freezer bags. Serve as smoked fish or combine fish with cream cheese, lemon juice, garlic and paprika to make spread.

Robert Seidles
Downey, Indiana

Heather Ann's Fish And Chips

Serves: 4
Prep Time: 15 minutes

1	**lb. fish fillets (walleye, perch or bluegill), cut into 2-inch pieces**
	vegetable oil
4-5	**potatoes, cut into 1/2-inch wedges**
1	**cup flour**
1/2	**tsp. salt**
1/2	**tsp. baking soda**
1	**T. malt vinegar**
1	**cup cold water**

Heat vegetable oil in deep-fat fryer to 350 degrees and fry 1/4 of potato wedges at a time for 5-7 minutes; separate potatoes with long-handled fork. Drain and put on cookie sheet covered in aluminum foil in warm oven while preparing fish. Rinse fish and pat with paper towel to dry. Combine flour, salt, baking soda, vinegar and water to form batter. Dip fish into batter. Fry 5-6 pieces at a time for about 3 minutes, turning fish once while frying. Drain fillets on paper towels and place on foil-lined cookie sheet in warm oven. When all fillets are fried, remove from oven. Broil potatoes in oven for 3 minutes until crisp. Sprinkle vinegar and salt over potatoes. (Apple wedges or onion rings may be substituted for potatoes.)

Kevin Pfaff
Ripon, Wisconsin

Harry's Fish Breading

Serves: several
Prep Time: 30-45 minutes

	fish fillets	**1**	**tsp. garlic salt**
1	**cup unbleached flour**	**1-2**	**tsp. chili powder**
1	**cup buttermilk pancake**	**3**	**tsp. baking powder**
	mix		**cooking oil**
2	**tsp. garlic powder**		

Soak fish fillets in water. Combine remaining ingredients in plastic bag and shake to mix. Put fillets in plastic bag, shaking to coat. Chill in refrigerator. Heat oil in skillet; add fillets one at a time, turning once.

Harry Shore
Corning, New York

Fishhead Soup

Serves: 5
Prep Time: 45 minutes

5	**lbs. fishheads**	**1/2**	**tsp. garlic salt**
3	**lbs. potatoes, diced**		**pepper to taste**
1 1/2	**lbs. carrots, diced**	**1**	**small can evaporated**
2	**lbs. onions, diced**		**milk**
1	**tsp. tarragon**	**1/4**	**lb. butter or margarine**

Boil fish to loosen gills, bones and eyes. Put fish and stock in separate containers and let stand. In saucepan, combine potatoes, carrots and onions; add enough water to cover. Cook vegetables at moderate heat for 15 minutes, adding water if needed. Add fish and seasonings and cook for 5 minutes. Add evaporated milk and butter; simmer for 20 minutes.

John O'Toole
Alamo, Texas

Padre's Fish Chowder

Serves: 8-10
Prep Time: 45 minutes

2	lbs. fish, diced	1	tsp. salt	
4	lbs. potatoes, diced into 1/2-inch squares	1	tsp. pepper	
		2 1/2	lbs onions, diced	
1	tsp. tarragon	1/4	cup butter or margarine	
1	tsp. curry			
1 1/2	cups evaporated milk			

Put diced potatoes in kettle and cover with water. Add spices, boiling for 5 minutes. Add onion and boil for an additional 15 minutes. Add fish and boil for 8-10 minutes. Reduce heat to simmer; stir in butter and add milk. If necessary, turn up heat and continue stirring until chowder reaches desired temperature.

John O'Toole
Alamo, Texas

Dough Dip

Serves: 4-6
Prep Time: 45 minutes

4-6	fish fillets	1	T. onion powder	
1/2	cup grits (sifted)	1/2	T. garlic powder	
1/2	cup white, unbleached flour		salt to taste	
3	eggs or	1/4	cup milk	
4	egg whites		oil	

Combine grits, flour, eggs, seasonings and milk to form batter. Add more milk if necessary. Dip fish into batter to coat. Deep-fry in oil at 375 degrees until fillets are golden brown. Drain fish on paper towels and serve.

Harry Shore
Corning, New York

Beer-Battered Fish

Serves: 4
Prep Time: 30 minutes

2   lbs. fish, cut into 1-inch-thick chunks
1   cup flour
1   12-oz. bottle beer
1   T. paprika
¹/₂ tsp. salt
**   cooking oil**

Combine flour, beer and seasonings to form batter. Dip fish chunks into batter and fry a few pieces at a time in deep-fat fryer at 375 degrees for 1-2 minutes. Cook fish until batter is golden brown. Remove fish chunks from oil, drain on paper towels and serve.

Philip Duval
Medical Lake, Washington

Baked Cheese Cracker Fish Fillets

Serves: 4
Prep Time: 45 minutes

4-5 fish fillets
2   cups cheese crackers, crushed
3-4 T. corn oil

Preheat oven to 350 degrees. On bottom of cookie sheet, place sheet of aluminum foil large enough to fold over fillets. Crush cheese crackers with rolling pin in paper bag. Pour corn oil into bowl and dip fillets into oil. Put fillets into bag of crushed crackers and shake to coat. Place coated fillets on cookie sheet and fold foil over fish. Bake for 35 minutes. Open foil and bake another 5 minutes to brown fillets. Serve.

Alfred Welch
Lyons, Kansas

Simple Baked Fish

Serves: several
Prep Time: 40-45 minutes

> **fish fillets**
> **1 pkg. onion soup mix**
> **salt and pepper to taste**

Season one side of fillets with onion soup mix (1 T. per fillet) and salt and pepper. Wrap fillets in aluminum foil and place on cookie tin. Bake at 350 degrees for 30 minutes.

Alan Shepherd
Gettysburg, Pennsylvania

Rolled Fish

Serves: several
Prep Time: 2 hours, 30 minutes

> **fish fillets**
> **green onions, chopped**
> **green peppers, chopped**
> **your favorite cheese, shredded or sliced**
> **bacon slices**
> **white wine**

Layer each fillet with onions, peppers and cheese. Roll fillet and wrap bacon slice around each fillet. Soak fillets in white wine for 2 hours. Bake or broil until bacon is crisp.

Tim Fogarty
Westland, Michigan

Pickled Fish

Serves: several
Prep Time: 3 days plus 1 hour

3 lbs. fish, skinned and cut into 1-inch chunks
1 cup non-iodized salt
4 cups water
white vinegar
onions, thinly sliced
lemons, thinly sliced

Pickling Mixture:
2 cups white vinegar
2 cups sugar
2 T. pickling spices
1 tsp. red pepper flakes

Mix non-iodized salt and water until salt is dissolved to form brine. Soak fish chunks in brine for 48 hours, stirring once each day. Drain brine from fish and rinse fish in cold water. Pour vinegar over fish and layer onion and lemon slices on top of fish. Soak fish for 24 hours. To make pickling mixture, combine vinegar and sugar with spices in saucepan. Bring mixture to a boil; cool. Spoon pickling mixture over fish in jars to within 1/8 inch of top. Place lemon slices and chopped onions on top of fish in jars. Seal jars with canning-style lids and store fish in refrigerator for 10 days before eating.

Smoked Fish

Serves: several
Prep Time: 9-10 hours

> **1   whole fish, gutted**
> **1   cup non-iodized salt**
> **1   cup brown sugar**
>   **soy sauce**

Combine salt and brown sugar. Sprinkle salt-sugar mixture inside fish cavity and on body of fish. With kitchen spray bottle, spray soy sauce inside fish cavity and on exterior of fish. Place fish in large bowl and refrigerate for 3 hours. Spray fish again with soy sauce inside and out. Smoke fish for 4-6 hours until done. (Time will vary depending upon size of fish.)

Smoked Fish Sandwich Spread

Serves: several
Prep Time: 20-25 minutes

> **2   cups smoked fish, finely flaked**
> **1/2 cup sharp cheddar cheese, grated**
> **1   can crushed pineapple**
> **1   cup mayonnaise**
>   **bread slices**
>   **butter**

Combine fish, cheese and crushed pineapple with enough mayonnaise to moisten. Spread mixture between slices of bread buttered on outside. Grill sandwiches until golden brown.

Leo Seffelaar
Tantallon, Saskatchewan

Index

BAKED FISH
A 'Dilly' Of A Perch, 169
A-Wards' Alaskan Halibut Supreme, 116
Baked Catfish, 29
Baked Mackerel Provencal, 125
Baked Pineapple Turbot, 237
Baked Trout, 227
Baked Whiting With Capers, 272
Basic Baked, 108
Best Stuffed Bass, 11
Bohemian Gypsy Carp, 26
Burgundy Baked Butterfish, 23
Cajun Baked Haddock, 87
Canadian/Cornish Fish Pasties, 205
Catfish Anna, 31
Cheesy Catfish, Please, 29
Chubby Checkers, 33
Cranberry-Stuffed Bass, 15
Creamy Asparagus Mahi Mahi, 127
Double Ocean Delite, 192
Easy Grouper With Broccoli, 84
Flavorful Stuffed Lingcod, 123
Foiled Flounder and Veggie Bake, 80
Grilled Or Baked Largemouth Bass, 10
Haddock Orange Onion Bake, 87
Herbed Salmon Terrine With Aspic, 186
Krispie Crappie, 213
Lemon-Rice Stuffed Salmon, 180
Maine Lobster Quiche, 69
Neptune's Favorite, 179
Northwest Petrale Sole, 193
Oven-Fried Flounder, 79
Oven-Fried Tilapia, 223
Pike—Or The Like—With Caper Sauce, 58
Quick Bake Pollock, 171
Red Fish On A Green Bed, 143
Salmon Lemon Loaf, 182
Seasoned Bake Tilefish, 225
Shad Cakes, 55
Simple Baked Fish, 278
Smelt Roma, 190

Stuffed Hake Fillets, 270
Stuffed Salmon, 184
Stuffed Sole Florentine, 193
Stuffed Trout With Bacon, 229
Tangy Baket Fillets, 145
Tender Baked Bass, 11
Tilapia Vegetable Bake, 223
Viva L'Tilapia, 224
Yankee Halibut, 118

BASS
Bass Fillets Piquant, 100
Best Stuffed Bass, 11
Broiled Sea Bass With Rarebit Sauce, 14
Cranberry-Stuffed Bass, 15
Deep-Fried Fish, 10
Garlic Broiled Bass, 16
Grilled Or Baked Largemouth Bass, 10
Grilled Sea Bass, 48
Micro-Easy Bianco Bass, 12
Micro-Easy Orange Butter Sea Bass, 13
Striped Bass On Buttered Crouttes, 53
Tender Baked Bass, 11

BLUEFISH
Fried Bluefish Fillets, 17
Grilled Bluefish With Vegetable Vinaigrette, 18
Micro-Easy Bay Blue Chowder, 17

BONITO
Bayland Brochettes, 20
Oriental Bonito Stir-Fry, 19
Quick Oven-Poached Bonito, 19

BROILED FISH
Bayland Brochettes, 20
Bass Fillets Piquant, 100
Broiled Breaded Grouper, 84
Broiled Lake Trout, 233
Broiled Sea Bass With Rarebit Sauce, 14
Broiled Shad, 56
Broiled Walleye With Mustard Sauce, 139
Garlic Broiled Bass, 16

Garlic Swordfish Broil, 222
Lemon-Garlic Perch, 169
Quick Broiled Butterfish With Lemon Glaze, 22
Salmon With Hollandaise Sauce, 181

BURBOT
Burbot Fish, 21

BUTTERFISH
Burgundy Baked Butterfish, 23
Quick Broiled Butterfish With Lemon Glaze, 22

CAJUN/CREOLE
Cajun Baked Haddock, 87
Catfish With Creole Sauce, 28
Micro-Easy Alhambra Creole, 76
Shrimp New Orleans Style, 77

CARP
Bohemian Gypsy Carp, 26
Carp Patties, 27
Carp Swimming In Sweet And Sour Sauce, 25
Gefilte Fish, 24

CATFISH
Baked Catfish, 29
Blackened Catfish, 105
Catfish Anna, 31
Catfish With Creole Sauce, 28
Cheesy Catfish, Please, 29
Micro-Easy Calico Catfish, 30

CHOWDER/SOUP
Boston Clam Chowder, 60
Carrot Soup, 205
Continental Clam & Corn Chowder, 155
Curried Trout Soup, 210
Fish & Potato Soup, 144
Fishhead Soup, 275
Flounder Chowder, 79
Italian Mullet Soup, 166
Key Conch Chowder, 157
Malabar Curried Trout Soup, 210
Manhattan Clam Chowder, 61
Micro-Easy Bay Blue Chowder, 17
Micro-Easy Classic Cod Chowder, 35
Micro-Easy Quick Shrimp Soup, 76
Padre's Fish Chowder, 276
Salmon Chowder, 258
Seafood Bisque, 147
Squid Chowder, 251

CHUB
Camper's Special, 32
Chubby Checkers, 33
Micro-Easy Creamed Chub With Capers, 32

COD
Bite-Sized Cod Balls, 34
Cathy's Pan-Fried Fish Parmesana, 36
Codfish Balls, 35
Easy Portuguese Cod, 34
Micro-Easy Classic Cod Chowder, 35
Smoked Black Cod And Mandarin Orange
    Salad, 255

CRAPPIE
Fried Fish, 65
Krispie Crappie, 213
Special Fried Crappie, 64
Steamed Crappies, 65

CROAKER
Easy Pan-Fried Croaker, 67
Wine-Spiced Croaker, 66

CRUSTACEANS
Boston Clam Chowder, 60
Champion Shrimp, 68
Classic Crab Louis, 71
Crab-A-Rama With Sauces, 74
Crayfish Dill, 104
Crayfish Kabobs, 75
Crayfish With Peppers, 75
Dressed Dungeness Crab, 256
Eggs Stuffed With Crab Meat, 58
Fish And Shrimp Crepes, 110
Fluffy King Crab Omelet, 72
Hot Lobster Ring, 68
King Crab Jambalaya, 73
Lobster Sauce, 47
Maine Lobster Quiche, 69
Manhattan Clam Chowder, 61
Mediterranean Fish Cioppino, 254
Micro-Easy Alhambra Creole, 76
Micro-Easy Lobster Newburg, 69
Micro-Easy Quick Shrimp Soup, 76
Savory Deviled Crab, 70
Seafood Bisque, 147
Sharon's Hot Crab Dip, 72
Shrimp In Garlic Butter, 78
Shrimp Kabobs, 102

Shrimp New Orleans Style, 77
Steamed Lobster, 48

DESSERTS
Apple Normandy, 111
Applesauce Pie With Whipped Cream, 142
Bread Pudding, 59
Burnt Cream, 216
Chocolate Fudge Cheese Cake, 206
Chocolate Upside Down Cake, 101
Chunky Apple Walnut Cake, 209
Coffee Nut Tortoni, 252
Cream Cheese Berry Pie, 255
Fresh Fruit Torte, 51
Ginger Fruit, 255
Grand Marnier Strawberry Mousse, 114
Lemon Syllabub, 54
Lime Ice, 261
Macadamia Nut Chocolate, 264
Mango Cream, 204
Oatmeal Orange Chocolate Chip Cookies, 144
Peach Melba, 48
Pear Pie, 140
Pier House Key-Lime Pie, 103
Pineapple Freeze, 214
Raspberry Champagne, 106
Red Chocolate Cake, 57
Rhubarb And Orange Crumble, 62
Sour Cream Chocolate Cake With Cream
    Cheese, 151
Strawberry Pecan Torte, 108
Strawberry Pie, 148
White Cake With Chocolate Pudding Frosting,
    146

FLOUNDER
Flounder Chowder, 79
Foiled Flounder and Veggie Bake, 80
Micro-Easy Florentine Flounder, 81
Oven-Fried Flounder, 79

FRIED FISH
Blackened Catfish, 105
Bluegill Oriental, 213
Carp Patties, 27
Carp Swimming In Sweet And Sour Sauce, 25
Cathy's Pan-Fried Fish Parmesana, 36
Codfish Balls, 35
Deep-Fried Fish, 10

Easy Pan-Fried Croaker, 67
Fab Fish Fritters, 102
Fried Bluefish Fillets, 17
Fried Fish, 65
Fried Grunion, 86
Grand Strand Fish Cakes, 172
Nutty Fried Trout, 208
Oven-Fried Flounder, 79
Sole Supreme With Avocado Sauce, 194
Southern Fish Fry A.K.A. Fish & Chips, 113
Special Fried Crappie, 64

FROGLEGS
Braised Froglegs, 82
Frog Bonne Femme, 82
Ol' South Froglegs, 83

GRILLED FISH
Classic Grilled Whiting, 271
Crayfish Kabobs, 75
Grilled Bluefish With Vegetable Vinaigrette, 18
Grilled Halibut With Biggie Butter, 258
Grilled Marinated Tuna With Pineapple Butter,
    236
Grilled Or Baked Largemouth Bass, 10
Grilled Shark With Ginger Glaze, 188
Grilled Sea Bass, 48
Grilled Trout Italiano, 234
Grilled Trout With Bacon And Vegetable
    Stuffing, 228
Mexicali Grilled Halibut, 117
Tandoori Salmon, 259
Whole Grilled Whitefish With Lime-Mint Butter,
    268

GROUPER
Broiled Breaded Grouper, 84
Easy Grouper With Broccoli, 84
Micro-Easy Sunshine Grouper Bake, 85

GRUNION
Fried Grunion, 86

HADDOCK
Cajun Baked Haddock, 87
Captain's Sauce For Pasta, 88
Haddock Orange Onion Bake, 87

HALIBUT
A-Wards' Alaskan Halibut Supreme, 116
Grilled Halibut With Biggie Butter, 258

Mexicali Grilled Halibut, 117
Micro-Easy Halibut Steaks, 118
Poached Alaskan Halibut With Cucumber
    Sauce, 119
Yankee Halibut, 118

ITALIAN
Captain's Sauce For Pasta, 88
Cathy's Pan-Fried Fish Parmesana, 36
Curried Clam Sauce For Pasta, 156
Grilled Trout Italiano, 234
Italian Mullet Soup, 166
Micro-Easy Pollock Italian Style, 171
Mussel Sauce With Pasta, 158

JACK
Jack Fillets Marinara, 121
Smoked Fish Pate Appetizers, 120

LINGCOD
Flavorful Stuffed Lingcod, 123
"Just In Thyme" Lingcod, 122
Lingcod Nicoise, 251
Micro-Easy Chinese Lingcod, 124

MACKEREL
Baked Mackerel Provencal, 125
Seafood Lovers Salad, 126
Spicy Steamed Mackerel, 125

MAHI-MAHI
Creamy Asparagus Mahi Mahi, 127
Luau Mahi Mahi, 127
Micro-Easy Pacific Island Fish, 128
Sweet And Sour Mahi Mahi, 128

MEXICAN
Enchilada Pesca, 203
Guacamole, 204
Mexicali Grilled Halibut, 117
Spanish Rice, 203

MICROWAVED FISH
Micro-Easy Alhambra Creole, 76
Micro-Easy Avocado Tuna Melt, 236
Micro-Easy Bay Blue Chowder, 17
Micro-Easy Bianco Bass, 12
Micro-Easy Calico Catfish, 30
Micro-Easy Chinese Lingcod, 124
Micro-Easy Classic Cod Chowder, 35
Micro-Easy Coquille St. Jacques, 163

Micro-Easy Creamed Chub With Capers, 32
Micro-Easy Deep Sea Delite, 178
Micro-Easy Florentine Flounder, 81
Micro-Easy Halibut Steaks, 118
Micro-Easy Herbed Swordfish Steaks, 222
Micro-Easy Light Sea Trout, 231
Micro-Easy Lobster Newburg, 69
Micro-Easy Mullet Magic, 167
Micro-Easy Orange Butter Sea Bass, 13
Micro-Easy Oyster Saute, 161
Micro-Easy Pacific Island Fish, 128
Micro-Easy Pollock Italian Style, 171
Micro-Easy Quick Shrimp Soup, 76
Micro-Easy Sturgeon Stuffed Manicotti, 219
Micro-Easy Sunshine Grouper Bake, 85
Micro-Easy Yogurt Fish Fillets, 269
Nuked Walleye, 239

MISCELLANEOUS
Asparagus With Basil Vinaigrette Dressing, 208
Baked Cheese Cracker Fish Fillets, 277
Basic Baked, 108
Basque-Style Paella, 215
Beer-Battered Fish, 277
Bluegill Oriential, 213
Brandy Dilled Carrots, 146
Broiled Shad, 56
Broccoli Salad, 105
Broccoil Flowerettes With Black Bean Sauce,
    263
Butter Lettuce With Walnut Vinaigrette, 50
Canadian/Cornish Fish Pasties, 205
Chinese Lemon Fish, 262
Chutney Eggs, 259
Creamy Red Potato Mash, 151
Cucumber Salad, 143
Curried Mayonnaise Dipping Sauce, 189
Dough Dip, 276
Eggs Stuffed With Crab Meat, 58
Enchilada Pesca, 203
Fab Fish Fritters, 102
Fettuccini With Gorgonzola Sauce, 252
French-Canadian Fish, 150
Fish In Beer, 147
Fishhead Soup, 275
Fish & Potato Soup, 144
Fish And Shrimp Crepes, 110
Fried Bananas, 103

Guacamole, 204
German Mushroom Salad, 58
Golden-Fried Artichoke Hearts, 99
Green Beans Side Dish, 48
Gruyere Onion Corn Bread, 106
Harry's Fish Breading, 275
Heather Ann's Fish And Chips, 274
Heaven & Earth, 59
Homemade Garlic Croutons, 108
Hot French Bread Cheese Rolls, 143
'Hot' Soy Dipping Sauce, 242
Hot Spinach And Bacon Salad, 52
Hungarian Potato Cakes, 148
Irish Soda Bread, 209
Jack's Red Dipping Sauce, 64
Lemon Butter-Dill Brussels Sprouts, 142
Lemon-Parsley Rice, 145
Mandarin Orange And Almond Salad, 211
Mashed Rutabagas, 100
Mediterranean Fish Cioppino, 254
Molded Fish Fillets, 272
Oven-Smoked Fish, 273
Padre's Fish Chowder, 276
Pickled Fish, 279
Pilaf With Curry Dressing, 260
Pita Rounds, 261
Plain Tomato Salad, 213
Poppy-Seed Coleslaw, 112
Potatoes With Tomato Sauce, 141
Quenelles, 47
Red Fish On A Green Bed, 143
Roe Salad Maryland, 55
Rolled Fish, 278
Romaine Salad With Strawberries, 99
Sauted Garlic Mushrooms, 52
Seafood Bisque, 147
Shad Cakes, 53
Shad Roe With Toast, 60
Simple Baked Fish, 278
Sliced Zucchini, 206
Smoked Fish, 280
Smoked Fish Cheese Ball, 50
Smoked Fish Sandwich Spread, 280
Snapper Hot Sauce, 192
Southern Fish Fry A.K.A. Fish & Chips, 113
Spanish Rice, 203
Spinach Caesar Salad, 109

Spinach Pasta With Smoked Fish And Cream
     Sauce, 51
Spinach Salad With Burgundy Dressing, 149
Sweet Sesame Sour Dipping Sauce, 241
Tangy Baked Fillets, 145
Tomato & Onion Salad With Vinaigrette, 139
Tomato Basil Dipping Sauce, 190
Walnut Basil Salad, 107
Wild Rice Side Dish, 48

MOLLUSKS
7 Seas Stuffed Peppers, 162
Abalone Balls, 154
Bay Island Fritters, 158
Chesapeake Clams Appetizer, 156
Clam And Spinach Canapes, 257
Continental Clam & Corn Chowder, 155
Curried Clam Sauce For Pasta, 156
Deep-Fried Calamari, 154
Easy Baked Oysters, 160
Fried Squid Rings, 165
Key Conch Chowder, 157
Mediterranean Stuffed Squid, 164
Micro-Easy Coquille St. Jacques, 163
Micro-Easy Oyster Saute, 161
'Mussel' In On The Stew, 158
Mussel Sauce With Pasta, 158
Scallops With Wine And Garlic, 214
Traditional Oysters Rockefeller, 160
Vinaigrette Style Mussels With Sauce, 159

MULLET
Italian Mullet Soup, 166
Micro-Easy Mullet Magic, 167
Mullet A La Palm Beach, 166

ORIENTAL
Breaded Sweet And Sour Fish, 229
Chinese Lemon Fish, 262
Carp Swimming In Sweet And Sour Sauce, 25
Micro-Easy Chinese Lingcod, 124
Oriental Bonito Stir-Fry, 19
Sweet And Sour Mahi Mahi, 128
Swordfish Stir-Fry, 221

PERCH
A 'Dilly' Of A Perch, 168
Lemon-Garlic Perch, 168
Perch-Stuffed Artichokes, 169

PIKE
Northern Pike, 170
Pike—or The Like—With Caper Sauce, 58

POLLOCK
Grand Strand Fish Cakes, 172
Micro-Easy Pollock Italian Style, 171
Quick Bake Pollock, 171

POMPANO
Creamed Pompano, 173
Fish In A Skillet, 174
Whole Baked Pompano, 173

ROCKFISH
Flavorful Rockfish With Grapes, 176
Poached Garden Rockfish, 175

ROUGHY
Fish Lorraine, 177
Micro-Easy Deep Sea Delite, 178
Neptune's Favorite, 179

SALMON
Chris' Lemon Salmon, 187
Creamed Salmon On Toast, 141
Easy Court Bouillon, 187
Elegant Salmon Mousse, 185
Fried Fish, 182
Herbed Salmon Terrine With Aspic, 186
Lemon-Rice Stuffed Salmon, 180
Poached Salmon With Watercress Sauce, 183
Salmon Lemon Loaf, 182
Salmon Pate, 181
Salmon With Hollandaise Sauce, 181
Stuffed Salmon, 184
Tandoori Salmon, 259

SAUCES
Captain's Sauce For Pasta, 88
Curried Clam Sauce For Pasta, 156
Curried Mayonnaise Dipping Sauce, 189
'Hot' Soy Dipping Sauce, 242
Jack's Red Dipping Sauce, 64
Lemon-Tarragon Sauce, 113
Pecan Basil Dressing, 107
Snapper Hot Sauce, 192
Sweet Sesame Sour Dipping Sauce, 241
Tomato Basil Dipping Sauce, 190

SHARK
Grilled Shark With Ginger Glaze, 188
Summer Treat, 188

SMELT
Deep-Fried Smelt, 189
Smelt Into Sardines, 191
Smelt Roma, 190
Sticky Smelt, 253

SNAPPER
Double Ocean Delite, 192
Tex-Mex Steamed Snapper, 191

SOLE
Northwest Petrale Sole, 193
Sole Supreme With Avocado Sauce, 194
Stuffed Sole Florentine, 193

STEAMED
Spicy Steamed Mackerel, 125
Steamed Crappies, 65
Steamed Lobster, 48
Tex-Mex Steamed Snapper, 191

STURGEON
Beer-Battered Sturgeon, 218
Micro-Easy Sturgeon Stuffed Manicotti, 219
Smoked Sturgeon Cakes, 220
Smoked Sturgeon Pita Spread, 218

SWORDFISH
Garlic Swordfish Broil, 222
Micro-Easy Herbed Swordfish Steaks, 222
Seafood Kabobs, 221
Swordfish Stir-Fry, 221

TILAPIA
Oven-Fried Tilapia, 223
Tilapia Vegetable Bake, 223
Viva L'Tilapia, 224

TILEFISH
Gulfshore Special, 226
Seasoned Bake Tilefish, 225
Tilefish With Orange Curry Sauce, 225

TROUT
Baked Trout, 227
Basil-Baked Sea Trout, 230

Breaded Sweet And Sour Fish, 229
Broiled Lake Trout, 233
Grilled Trout Italiano, 234
Grilled Trout With Bacon And Vegetable
    Stuffing, 228
Micro-Easy Light Sea Trout, 231
Nutty Fried Trout, 208
Papa's Trout, 211
Priest Lake Smoke Trout, 233
Saginaw Bay Trout Salad, 231
Sea Trout A La Delmonico, 232
Smoked Trout Dip, 255
Stuffed Trout With Bacon, 229
Malabar Curried Trout Soup, 210
Trout Almandine, 230

TUNA
Basic Poached Tuna, 235
Grilled Marinated Tuna With Pineapple Butter,
    236
Micro-Easy Avocado Tuna Melt, 236
Tuna Dip, 235

TURBOT
Baked Pineapple Turbot, 237
Turbot Amandine, 237

WALLEYE
Broiled Walleye With Mustard Sauce, 139
Camper's Walleye Delight, 242
Gravy Walleye, 238
Nuked Walleye, 239
"Spiked" Pike, 240
Walleye Amandine, 238
Walleye Fillet Dijon, 240
Walleye Shore Lunch, 239
Whole Steamed Fish, 241

WHITEFISH
Great Lakes Special, 267
Milk-Poached Whitefish, 266
Quick Fish, 267
Stuffed Whitefish, 266
Whole Grilled Whitefish With Lime-Mint Butter,
    268

WHITING
Baked Whiting With Capers, 270
Cape Cod Salad, 271
Classic Grilled Whiting, 271
Micro-Easy Yogurt Fish Fillets, 269
Portuguese Whiting, 269
Stuffed Hake Fillets, 270

Contributing Members

Dean Auger
Gladstone, MI, 266

A.W. Akers
Knoxville, TN, 229

Bruce Bouvia
Astoria, OR, 193

Andrew Banchanski
Edison, NJ, 17

Gary Brookshire
Norman, IN, 233

Philip Duval
Medical Lake, WA, 277

Tim Fogarty
Westland, MI, 278

John Gagliardo
Oxnard, CA, 35, 86

David Gardner
Menasha, WI, 218

LeRoy Geist
Glasgow, MT, 239

David Glossenger
Honesdale, PA, 16, 170

Bernard Hardesty
Chico, CA, 154

Jeff Huelsman
LaVerne, CA, 127

Oscar Ison
Baker City, OR, 229

Sarah King
Wagoner, OK, 27

Joseph Kozlowski
Nemacolin, PA, 228, 234

R. Christopher Mathis
York, PA, 187

Bette Montag
Omaha, NE, 181

John O'Toole
Alamo, TX, 68, 227, 238, 239, 275, 276

Kevin Pfaff
Ripon, WI, 274

Paul Pirrello
Rockford, IL, 240

Thomas Schaad
Leawood, KS, 10, 29, 65

Steve Schlerf
Hydesville, CA, 36

Leo Seffelaar
Tantallon, SK, 15, 21, 26, 280

Robert Seidles
Downey, IN, 272, 273

Patricia Severe
Kenai, AK, 119

Alan Shepherd
Gettysburg, PA, 230, 278

Harry Shore
Corning, NY, 275, 276

Jack Smart
Clam Gulch, AK, 180, 182

Richard Street Jr.
Lac du Flambeau, WI, 235

Daniel Tatomer
Romulus, MI, 189, 242

Robert Ward
Anchor Point, AK, 116

Donald Warren
Lompoc, CA, 267

Alfred Welch
Lyons, KS, 277

Al Wirwas
Chatsworth, CA, 182